CW01627931

DESIGN FOR LIFE

Peter Jamieson

Some names have been changed in the writing of this book to respect the privacy of certain individuals.

ISBN: 978-0-9562879-4-6

Teeniemaleek Publications
Castletown
Caithness
KW14 8TP
Scotland
United Kingdom

To Frankie and Agnes

CONTENTS

ACKNOWLEDGEMENTS

I would like, first of all, to thank Chris Nicolson for her invaluable help in writing this book and for the times of encouragement, when unknown to her I have dearly needed them. I would also like to thank my dear friend, John Jarret, not only for his help in the writing of this book and his design work on the cover, but for his brotherly love, which although at times has been tough, I've always found to be beneficial. (Just you keep telling it like it is, John.)

Many thanks must, of course, go to my family. First of all to Vera, who has been an absolute rock throughout my life, whose love for me has never changed; to my brother, Norman, and his wife, Elizabeth, for their friendship and support; and to my son, Jamie, as well as his mother, Nicola, for making me feel so very welcome, especially considering how little contact we have had over the years.

Thanks, also, to the many friends who have stuck by me through thick and thin; Bryden Goodlad, Carol Polson, Alastair Inkster, as well as those more recently acquainted, who continue to support me in many different ways; Andy and Sabina, Karen Thomson, Jamie Tonge, Frank Miller, to name but a few. Your friendship towards me has been overwhelming. Thanks, guys.

There are, of course, many more names I could add here, and I am truly thankful to each and every one of them (you know who you are). However, I would like now to pay homage to the One who made all this possible, whose love for me has not only changed my life and inspired the writing of this story, but continues to bless me each day in ways that never cease to amaze me – Jesus Christ. To Him be all glory and honour, forever and ever. Amen.

INTRODUCTION

My name is John Jarrett and at the time of first meeting Peter I was a Drugs and Alcohol Support Worker at the Papa Stour Project in Shetland. As you read further into this book, you will find out more about the project and Peter's time there – which is but a brief part of his life, journey and this book, but an extremely pivotal time, too.

So why is the introduction of this autobiography being written by me?

I count Peter as one of my closest friends, having worked, lived, walked and struggled with him for five years. However, the reason I am writing is more to do with the unique position I held in Peter's life at a time of dramatic change, the observations that I had, as well as the conclusions I came to, and the shear level of amazement at how wrong I was proved to be.

When I first interviewed Peter for a place at the Project, my initial impression was that he had completely unrealistic expectations of turning around 25 years of living a life of drugs, alcohol and crime in four weeks, which was the maximum time he was willing to stay. There was no good reason to deny him a place at the project, although during that first interview at CADSS main office in Lerwick (Community Alcohol & Drugs Services Shetland) I very nearly did, as over the years I have found my initial impressions rarely to be wrong.

Without this becoming my autobiography, too, I have to give some background information to qualify the previous statement. I grew up in the East End of London in the late Seventies and Eighties and spent most of the first 25 years of my life caught up in crime, drugs and the seediest side of life. I was involved in gangs and drugs from a very early age; I did my first custodial sentence at the age of 15 after a stint in local authority care, and I soon found my way into drug dealing, prostitution and fraud. I can't remember a time since the age of 12 that I wasn't looking over my shoulder, as violence was never far away.

During a time of personal turmoil I asked Jesus into my life and became a Christian – a long story. Well, the truth is I asked God (whoever He was) for help when I had nowhere else to turn and He pointed me to Jesus. From that time on my life took a very different direction and for the best part of 19 years I have worked with homeless people in Central London and the south coast of England.

My work has brought me into close contact with thousands of people suffering from extreme forms of drug and alcohol misuse and mental health issues. A career path took me from working as a temporary night porter in a hostel for single homeless men to middle management affecting local authority poverty policies and voluntary sector support services for the most vulnerable in society. I only share this so you have an idea of my perspective concerning Peter.

I stated my initial opinion of Peter and his chances of success, which were somewhere between 0 – 2 %. This was an instinctive view based on 12 years of experience working with people in Peter's situation. I was by no means optimistic, but I was always hopeful and very willing to be proved wrong.

During the four weeks I spent with Peter at the Papa Stour Project, my initial opinion of him was this: Peter had damage to his brain from the years of abuse, nothing much had really changed, and even though his state of mind seemed more positive, his expectations for the future and the direction he wanted his life to take were very unrealistic. Therefore, my hope for a long-term recovery was virtually zero. I can remember everything in me wishing he would stay longer at the project, as I didn't want to witness the disaster that would undoubtedly follow his departure. I gave him less than a month.

What was to follow was nothing but a miracle, which really is the only word for it.

The exit plan one would prepare with any person leaving a drug and alcohol project, anywhere in the world, would have certain "no-nos" as a given. Peter, however, decided on his own exit plan that would follow a course of choices that broke every single "no-no" laid down before him. Yet over the following six months – and the years to come – I watched Peter go from strength to strength in his recovery from a lifetime of alcohol and drug abuse. I also saw changes in his attitudes and personality, which were all for the better, it has to be said. God did something miraculous in his life.

This is a truly enjoyable, humorous and often extremely revealing book about an amazing life transformed in an amazing Godly way, but in considering what to touch on in this introduction, I felt somewhat drawn to think more about what had not been said. In fact, I wanted to focus more on what seems to be largely omitted from most, if not all, Christian testimony books about changed lives – largely, I believe, due to the humility of the authors.

As Christians we believe it is God Who brings about the change in our lives, a truth we believe is beyond question. But this belief poses a question, one that Peter highlights in this book: "If it is God Who brings about the change, why doesn't everyone who goes through a Christian project, or church, have their lives so dramatically changed?" It's a question I have asked myself for many years.

The answer really is quite simple. How much does someone *want* God to change them? I know you are thinking, 'Okay, so people don't change because they don't want it enough, so it's not down to God really, but the person'. Controversially, the answer is yes, that's right. But when this question, and more importantly the answer, is understood properly, there really is no controversy.

Too many Christian organisations, churches and well-meaning Christians only tell part of the story. You see, God makes the change, but they forget to mention the *cost.* When we talk about people wanting to change, we are not talking about a desire, wish, hope, want or a feeling, perhaps; what we are really talking about is an action or, more accurately, a series of actions. It is not how much you desire it in your heart – although this is the birthplace of all motivation – but how willing you are to be led and, most of all, be obedient to what God asks you to do to bring about the change. How many times are you willing to make the right choice?

As I have watched Peter and walked with him over the years, I have seen the times of trial, of temptation, of self-denial, of discipline, of obedience. There have been times of great courage, of facing fear, humiliation, possible loss of relationships and loss of friendships, just to touch on a few. There have also been many times of poverty, frustration and loneliness, and times where Peter has desperately needed the support and wisdom of other Christians.

Throughout it all, as hard as it undoubtedly has been at times, he has consistently believed that God loves him, is leading him down a road to a better, fuller life, and that God only wants the best for him. This is what is meant by wanting it enough, being willing to choose God over and above everything, not choosing our old ways and old lives. These are the truths that are not always made clear to new believers. God/Jesus leads – but are we truly willing to follow when we face and understand the cost? Peter is, and does.

I hope you enjoy this book as much as I have, and as you read it, please pray, firstly for all the broken people you will come across in these pages, for those you know heading down a similar path, and for Peter. If you're reading this book and don't know God, Jesus – maybe you don't even believe there is such a being – all I ask is that you read with an open mind and listen to the words of one wiser than I.

John Jarrett
May, 2012

CHAPTER 1

It was Tuesday, June 3, 2008, and I was visiting the dentist in Lerwick with the hope of having a couple of teeth filled. The lady behind the reception desk – who obviously had no idea what it was like to have toothache, especially the kind I had – handed me a form to fill out as I waited.

What is it about people and forms? I thought. *It's all I ever seem to be doing these days. Can she not see how much pain I'm in?*

Finding a seat as far away from everyone else as possible, I sat down and glanced quickly over the list of questions, noticing that it was almost identical to the one I had already filled out three or four months before, when I first registered with this surgery.

"Why are they asking me these questions again?" I grumbled under my breath.

I set the form down on my lap and considered what I had written previously, wondering if I had perhaps made some sort of mistake, and then, drawing on my new found resolve, I briefly prayed and duly obliged. (It turned out that they were simply updating their files.)

Putting pen to paper I proceeded to fill in my name, address, occupation and so on, until I arrived at a section on my medical history, which asked if I had suffered from various illnesses or had any allergies. I looked down the seemingly endless list and automatically began ticking all of the "No" boxes, until I came to a question I sometimes found so difficult: "Do you have, or have you ever had, any of the following?"

It then listed about half a dozen blood infections, and right there, at the end, was my old friend, hepatitis C.

It shouldn't have been a hard question to answer really. After all, there were only ever two boxes to choose from: "Yes" or "No". But if you happen to have had hep C, or have it, or suspect you *might* have it, then it's a little different.

You see, for many years I had denied to myself that I might be hep C positive. In fact, I will have to admit to a couple of things here that are a little unsavoury. For instance, I had for a long time suspected that I might have hep C, but I still proceeded to have sexual relationships. I mean, I didn't know for certain, and I tried to avoid sexual encounters as best I could, but with the kind of people I hung around with, that was much easier said than done.

Then there was the odd occasion I needed medical treatment, like the time I filled out a form to join a private dentist in Aberdeen, just to have some emergency work done. Even though I knew there was a distinct possibility that I was carrying the virus, when faced with this same question I simply pushed it from my mind and ticked the "No" box.

I think by denying the possibility that I might be HIV and/or hep C positive, I thought it just wouldn't happen to me. Regardless of the situations I found myself in – when there was a very real chance of spreading it to others – I just didn't want to know, and what's more, I was never in any hurry to find out either.

Yet a lot had changed since those days of irresponsibility, as I had now learned the answer to that question: "Do you have, or have you ever had, hepatitis C?", and the last time I was there filling out a similar form, I very sadly had to tick the "Yes" box.

Ticking that box after all those years of uncertainty had been a difficult thing to do, not because I had been overly worried about it, but because of the many implications it involved. For instance, how many others possibly had hep C as a result of my actions? Who should I be informing about it? How long had I been walking around with it in my system and to a certain degree knowingly putting other people's lives at risk? Why hadn't I faced up to this possibility sooner?

Yes, this seemingly simple question – did I or did I not have hep C – had plagued me for long enough, and just when I had become used to the idea that I had it, as well as having painstakingly dealt as best I could with the implications involved, the situation had again changed. It now required a little more thought.

So I decided I would leave that question for the time being and proceed to the next lot of questions, which were, at least, a little more fun to answer.

"Are you a smoker?"

"How many cigarettes do you smoke in a day?"

"How many units of alcohol do you drink in a week?"

The one concerning alcohol was particularly amusing to me. It was a multiple choice question offering differing amounts that seemed to range from "totally irrelevant" to "not much more than a good day out".

I put a tick in the "No" box concerning smoking and then looked again at the one about alcohol. I glanced around the waiting area to see if anyone was watching me fill out my form but, sadly, no one was. And so, with a cheeky sort of grin on my face, I scribbled down "None".

Oh, come on now! How many people can actually do that these days? Not a lot, I'm sure! But the truth of the matter was I took great pride in writing that; to me it was a big deal. So much so, in fact, that if I had managed to catch someone's eye in that waiting area I would have asked, and rather smugly, too, "See that question about alcohol and how many units you drink in a week ...? Do you think it would be better to put down a zero, or just write 'none'?" Just so they all knew.

But as much as I would have enjoyed that, the truth is it hadn't always been that way.

* * *

In June 2006, I was in a drugs rehabilitation unit on a tiny island called Papa Stour in the Shetland Isles. I was 38 years old and had suffered off and on with varying degrees of alcoholism, along with drug addiction, for what by then had been the greatest part of my adult life, causing many problems throughout.

Initially, I had gone there on the advice of a few close friends and my older sister, Vera, as well as those working with me at the Community Alcohol and Drugs Services Shetland (CADSS) to try to help me sustain a recovery after successfully completing a detox programme. It was certainly one of the best decisions I have ever made.

For over 20 years I had struggled with both alcoholism and drug addiction. In fact, I truly never thought I would see a day when I wouldn't be doing, if not both, at least one of those things. Yet, after a brief spell on Papa Stour, I don't feel the need to drink every day and I certainly don't desire drugs. Hey, I even stopped smoking!

I think back on it all now and still can't believe that I used to be that person. Just so much has changed in my life. It truly is incredible, and things just keep on happening to me as a result! Good things, amazing things – miracles, even!

Yes, I have had many miracles happen to me since my time in Papa Stour and as I sat there that afternoon in the dentist's waiting area, waiting patiently on a dentist to put me out of my misery – which considering my track record with dentists was another miracle really – I couldn't help but think back to how it all began.

What was it that made a young Lerwick boy turn out the way he did? Was there any connection between alcohol and drug addiction? Was there ever any indication from a young age that things might end up the way they did? Could it all have been avoided? I wasn't sure, to be honest, and doubted I would ever find an answer, but it was certainly worth considering, nonetheless. How did it all begin?

* * *

My use of alcohol only really began to be a problem when at about the age of 16, having been kicked out of school – and after a brief spell working in one of the local fish factories – I went off to work in an old meat market.

The Shetland Marts, or "da Marts", as the locals used to call it, was a mixture of a few things. It was a wholesale fresh meat and frozen food suppliers; it had a sale ring for the auction of livestock; there were sheds filled with sheep and cattle pens and a furniture auction room, which held sales every Tuesday afternoon. It even held the occasional barn dance, of all things. From frozen sweetcorn to sheep's heads, from kettles to cars, it pretty much sold everything you could think of, and probably a heck of a lot more besides! (Especially once I started working there, when cannabis could be added to that list.)

Sadly, this building no longer exists. It was razed to the ground some years ago and replaced by a supermarket, but it really had to be seen to be believed. It was dirty, it was falling down, and it only ever survived being condemned year after year by means of a backhander to one or two local officials at the Health and Safety Department, allegedly.

I can remember, like it was yesterday, my first day in that grotty, old meat market. I recall being so nervous that morning that I very nearly never made it. If it hadn't been for my mother's persistence, and the fact that I was supposed to be filling in for my friend, Brian, while he was away on holiday, I doubt very much if I would have gone anywhere near the place. But, there I was, this skinny, little 16-year-old, who had not long been dragged out of bed by his mother, about to get his first real taste of work.

The first thing that I noticed, as I walked in the doors of da Marts, was the smell. It wasn't such a bad smell, mind you, just a mixture of sawdust, dead animals and blood, which was hardly surprising when it was all around you. There were sides of beef that hung on hooks from the ceiling; there were quarter cuts of beef lining one wall and along the other a row of steel worktops, which were used to further process the meat. Then, of course, there were the chilled rooms, which were quite often packed wall to wall with lamb carcasses, sides of pigs and trays of offal.

Yes, the old meat market had a very distinctive smell, indeed, and it was also extremely noisy. There was the hum-drumming of an industrial mincer constantly grinding away inside the main door; there was the incessant screeching of a bandsaw in the far corner, ripping through carcasses as if they were made of cheese, and there was the rather jovial sound of those hardy, local butchers, as they brightened up their day by poking fun at someone, usually me.

In some respects it was a pretty awful place, but I just loved it. I loved the look and the smell of that old meat market, the brashness of the people who worked there and strangely enough, I enjoyed the actual work itself.

My duties, I suppose, were quite simple. I fetched, carried, did as I was told – well, most of the time – and at the end of each afternoon I took apart and washed all the machinery. There were certain jobs in that place that were just mine, and I made them very much my own, learning to do each one efficiently and taking great pride in it, too.

There were also plenty of interesting little jobs that took you outside of da Marts. For instance, I might go out in the truck and help collect the lamb carcasses from the slaughter house, or I might go and help with the live sales at the auction, transferring sheep and cattle from their pens into the ring and hosing it all down afterwards. Even collecting old furniture from people's houses for the weekly sale was a job I often undertook. There was no end to the different kinds of jobs I might be expected to do in the course of a day, but they all suited me just fine. It was simply a case of hard, physical work, which for someone who had completely flunked school like I had – and didn't really have the confidence to tackle anything too mentally challenging – was fine by me.

When those first couple of weeks were almost over, as Brian was about to return from his holidays, I was in for a major surprise. Completely out of blue I was offered a full-time job. Hughie Johnson, the foreman at the time, asked me into the office and with one of his big, toothless grins, told me what a good worker they all thought I was, how much everyone had enjoyed having me around, and that a permanent position within the company was mine if I wanted it.

I remember being absolutely astounded and surprisingly quite moved, not because I had been offered a job, but because someone had actually said something positive over me. Of course, I gladly accepted the offer and not because of the fun I was having; rather, for once in my life I felt appreciated for who I was and what I could do.

That had actually been quite a new experience. Someone had identified a use for me, thought I was good at something and wanted me around, unlike at home, and more so at school, where I was always looked upon as being rather hopeless.

That was the start of my working life and one of only two proper jobs I think I ever had. I ended up working there for about three years, before finally giving it up to pursue a career in drug dealing, but it was three years that helped shape me into what I was to become for most of my adult life – an alcoholic.

* * *

You see, alcohol and Shetland are like Siamese twins. They are intrinsically entwined as if their lives depend upon each other, with everything that goes on basically governed by drink. There is hardly a social occasion on this island, of which I am aware, where the focus doesn't eventually turn to alcohol, and that can be said of most family situations, too. Whether it's a wedding, a birthday, or just a day when you have the family round for dinner, alcohol quickly becomes the focus for everyone.

Now, I am sure this isn't something unique to Shetland, by any means; in fact, I'm fairly positive that nearly every community in Britain will have a very similar story to tell. But Shetland, I do believe, is different in many ways. With its longer, colder, darker winters and its only too-brief summer months that barely reach double figures in degrees Celsius, any opportunity to party is usually a very welcome reprieve, indeed.

I was raised in a home that reflected this attitude and where socialising seemed to have priority. I won't say that working wasn't important, or that the general welfare of the family was in any way neglected, but everything was quiet and largely uninteresting unless, of course, there was something to celebrate.

Now, celebrating in our household took on many shapes and forms. It could be a visit from a neighbour, who just happened to be passing the door on their way home with their shopping, or perhaps a visit from a relative who lived out of town a little, or it might be that some Country and Western band would be playing in the British Legion, or just simply that they fancied a party. Whatever the reason – if one was required – socialising was the thing to do.

Growing up with two older parents and a brother and sister, who were both in their mid-teens by the time I arrived, meant there was always something going on in our house. In fact, some of my fondest childhood memories are of the many parties that used to take place in our home. The music, the laughter, the pocket money! Yes, they could be quite rowdy affairs, often stretching way off into the following day, but for a young boy like me they were a lot of fun and a great opportunity to scam a few quid.

I suppose a lot of my parents' friends must have found it quite amusing that this little boy had suddenly appeared on the scene, especially when all of their own children had more than likely grown up and left home. I must admit that I was completely spoiled rotten by them all and totally revelled in the attention, which was made all the easier, as there was a party almost every weekend.

Friday would come and my parents would get ready to go out, the babysitter would arrive – usually a relative of some description or another – and after a few drams they would head off out to the bar. Then, much later at night or maybe sometime in the early hours of the morning, I would wake to the sound of Tammy Wynette, who was still "standing by her man". Or perhaps it would be the deep, gravel-sounding voice of Johnny Cash that raised me from my slumber, adamant that he'd have "the only one there is around".

I would usually lie a while, listening as everyone sang along, their voices getting louder and louder the drunker they became. And the drunker they became, sadly, the more out of tune it all would sound, until I was left with very little choice but to rise from my bed, go downstairs and attempt to join in the fun.

Yes, they certainly loved to have their little parties, and what was so wrong with that? I never saw anything in all my days as a child that was wrong in it. I saw the odd kiss out in the back garden or on the staircase, perhaps, between two people who were married to someone other than the person they were locking mouths with. I would quite often see men and women falling about drunk, or perhaps crying as they sang along to the odd song, but there was never any animosity or reason to believe that this was in any way wrong. No, my idea of alcohol as I grew up was that it was perfectly normal – and you wouldn't have fun without it!

And there, I suppose, lies the danger.

* * *

Not being a stranger to alcohol from such a young age meant I was bound to have my moments, and I certainly did. I remember, as a six-year-old, finding a carryout hidden underneath an old metal tank and sitting down to drink it with a friend, Neil, almost as if it was second nature to us ...

It was the day after the Lerwick Up-Helly-Aa, an annual fire festival held on the last Tuesday of January, where the people of Shetland get together to celebrate their Viking heritage. It largely involves a massive street procession and the burning of a replica Viking galley, intertwined with at least 48 hours of dancing and drinking, and whatever else might go on as a result.

Now, with it being a public holiday – Shetland being the only place in Britain that holds a holiday on this particular day, largely because no one is fit for work, even as late as midday – there was not a soul to be seen anywhere. There were no cars out on the roads, none of the shops were open, the schools were all closed and, due to the previous night's festivities, the majority of the town's adult population were either still in their beds or more than likely, after a 24-hour binge, just heading there.

Neil and I, being very much the opportunists, decided to take advantage of this once-a-year phenomenon to head off down into the docks for what we hoped would be an uninterrupted rummage around. We broke into one or two sheds, boarded a few fishing boats, smashed a couple of windows, ransacked a couple of council trucks and finished up at the back of Bolt's Garage, where we broke into one or two parked buses and managed to steal some loose change.

Disappointed at finding so little in the way of personal gain for such a golden opportunity as this day provided, as well as becoming a little bored with such mindless hooliganism, we decided to head for home.

On the way out of the docks, we stopped for a seat on some grass behind Garthspool Church, possibly to count out the money. We were just sitting there, talking away, when Neil suddenly rose up and scrambled in under this old water tank, which was raised a few feet off the ground.

I sat there watching him, wondering what on earth he was up to as he momentarily disappeared out of sight, until he came scurrying out again, backside first, dragging with him these two rather heavy carrier bags.

Knowing what was in them from the sound the bags were making as he half carried, half dragged them to where we had been sitting, we excitedly opened them. And what a surprise it was to find a bottle of whisky, a bottle of rum, half a dozen cans of Tennent's Lager – the ones with the half-naked women on the side – and half a dozen cans of McEwan's Export, known locally as "The Shetland Rose" because the empties are commonly found lying along grassy verges at the side of country roads.

Neil, who could only have been about five years old, grabbed the whisky and immediately twisted off the lid.

"My dad lets me drink whisky without any water in it!" he boasted, putting the bottle to his lips.

I knew he was lying, of course, but was most impressed, as he never even flinched. It was very convincing.

I opened a can of lager, had a few sips and then, feeling the need to impress, opened the bottle of rum, more to have a smell of it than anything else. But no sooner had I sniffed it than I began to sip it, a little at a time, unlike Neil who, I noticed, seemed to be gulping down the whisky.

And so the two of us just sat there, drinking away, as if it was something we did every day.

What happened after that, I can't quite recall, but I remember looking over at Neil, who was lying flat out on his back a few feet away from me, and noticing that the hands of the clock on Bolt's Garage had moved considerably, and also how cold it was. Well, it was January in Shetland, and by the time I woke up we were both lying in the shade rather than in the sunlight.

Deciding that it was time to leave, I stood up and tried to warm myself.

"Get up, Neil, we have to go now!" I called.

Standing there shivering, I looked over at Neil who hadn't moved. He just lay there, completely motionless, his eyes closed. Grabbing his arm, I began pulling him.

"Come on, Neil, you have to get up now!" I asserted.

But Neil just lay there, completely still.

"Look, if you don't get up now, I'll leave you and I'm not joking either!" I shouted, becoming annoyed.

As I stood looking down on him lying in a position where I could quite easily have poured beer on his face or stuck some grass up his nose, he didn't even bat an eyelid to see what I might be up to. So I began to kick him a little.

"Come on! Get up, Neil!" Kick. "Get up!" Kick. "Get up!" Kick. And so on it went for about a minute.

But Neil just wouldn't move or make a sound. Normally this highly-strung individual would have been up on his feet, attempting to give me a fat lip for the way I was treating him, but he just lay there with his eyes closed.

I shouted a couple more times, then made a decision to leave him. Staggering my way over to the back of Garthspool Church, I clambered up and over the wall, landing flat on my face on what would normally have been a street busy with pedestrians and cars. But it wasn't this afternoon; it was completely deserted, with just a lonely crisp bag blowing around in the corner of a wall, and the cries of some gulls as they fought over the remnants of someone's freshly-brought-up sick.

I picked myself up off the ground and looked back over the wall to where Neil lay, but to my annoyance he hadn't moved an inch.

"Look, I am going now, Neil, so I'll see you later. Okay?"

Still he didn't move.

By this time I was fed up with him and I walked off down the road, looking back every now and then, believing he would eventually come running after me.

Why isn't he following me? I thought. *Why isn't he chasing me down the road and racing me home?*

Eventually, after walking about a hundred yards, as far as Pete's sweetie shop, I stopped in my tracks, somehow knowing that I had to return.

So, back up the road I went, up and over the wall once more, only to find him exactly as I had left him minutes before. He simply hadn't moved in the slightest. In fact, on closer inspection, it didn't even look as if he was breathing.

I grabbed his arm and began to pull at him.

"Neil, you have to get up now!" I yelled. *"Get up!"*

I then knew that something was seriously wrong, and a horrible feeling came over me. To make matters worse, it seemed that the harder I tried to wake him, and the more desperate I became, the more impossible it was proving to be. He would only move about an inch every time I pulled at him, and the wall was a good 20 feet from where we were.

Suddenly, at the futility of my attempts to do something, I realised how hopeless it was. I just couldn't move him and he wasn't showing any signs of waking up. I sat down beside him and held his hand. His face was as white as snow.

"It's getting really late, Neil," I said, hoping to see a smile. I kept wishing he would open those blue eyes of his and laugh at me, but there was nothing. I started to cry.

"Neil! You have to get up. Oh, God, don't you bloody die! Please, God, please don't let him die, please ... *Please!*" I screamed.

Just then two men I had never seen before appeared out of nowhere, one on either side of me. They stood there for a moment or two, looking down at us, until one of the men bent down and gathered Neil up into his arms.

I was instantly filled with horror at how limp and lifeless he looked, how small and helpless he was in this man's arms. I suddenly sobered, as a chill ran right through me.

"Oh, God," I whimpered. "Please, don't be dead, Neil!"

Between them, the men managed to lift him up over the wall and then run with him the 200 yards or so down the road to North Lochside, where I'd told them we both lived. Within a minute or two we were outside Neil's house, and one of the men told me to go home.

I walked slowly backwards, watching them approach the door, and then hid around the corner to see what would happen. I saw Neil's mother appear behind the mottled glass panelling, then open the door to find two strange men standing before her, one of whom appeared to have the body of her only son draped across his arms. In that instant, all of my hopes quickly turned to dread. I turned and ran. With the palms of my hands pressed hard into my ears and that picture in my mind of his cold, white face, I ran and ran as fast as I could, trying with all of my might to outrun the screams of his poor mother ...

* * *

Yes, I certainly had many an encounter with alcohol during my childhood, but then again, that was the case with most of the children I grew up with. My situation wasn't unique in our neighbourhood, although I probably landed myself in a lot more trouble than most.

There was one night that a few of us broke into a warehouse that was used as a store by one of the local wholesale businesses and found all these bottles of champagne. Well, we took just about the whole lot – somewhere in the region of 500 bottles – and stashed them in my dad's shed, which, strangely, was the safest place to keep it, as no one really used it except me. We were all about 13 or 14 years old at the time, but that lot managed to keep us drunk for almost a whole year, with many a drunken incident resulting.

By the time I started working in the meat market, I was well established as a drinker. I was by no means an alcoholic – well, I didn't think so – certainly not compared to what I believed an alcoholic to be, but the influence da Marts had on me to drink shouldn't be underestimated.

I do have many happy memories of my time there; in fact, there was nowhere else really quite like it in the whole of Shetland. It was an amazing place to work and I'm glad to have been part of its history, but it definitely has a lot to answer for.

To the untrained eye, da Marts was just a wholesaler that specialised in meat, yet it was bursting with character in its own little way, with some truly great local characters: Mitney Grant, Hughie Johnson, Aald Lowrie, Jimmy Manson, Willie Tulloch, to name a few. But it was what went on behind the scenes in the little "back shop" that's of greatest interest to this story.

Yes, the back shop was where it all happened. It was a little room, just off the main work area, no more than 10 by 15 feet, with an adjoining room of roughly the same size, which was used as a tearoom.

Generally, the back shop was just somewhere to go if you fancied a smoke, or if you needed to get out of the cold for a while, but one of the main functions of this room was as a place to have a dram throughout the day and quite often entertain people. Now, you might think that a bit strange for an establishment like this, but a lot of entertaining went on in that little room.

Every afternoon, when the work was about done, usually around four o'clock, after having over rung the till by £20 or £30, the money would be extracted and a carryout bought from one of the nearby Off Licenses. This would normally consist of a bottle of whisky, a bottle of rum, and whatever was left over would be spent on lager.

As a 16-year-old, I thought it was great being handed a can of lager when I'd finished washing down all the machinery. There wasn't a night that I can remember, in the three or so years that I worked there, when that didn't happen, but it was all very sociable and always good fun.

Yes, I used to love those little parties in the back shop, and for those who were in the know outside of there, a good session was always to be had, especially on market days, which would have been an eye opener for even the hardest of drinkers.

At certain times of the year, da Marts was a venue where many of Shetland's crofters would meet together to sell their livestock, and at the same time catch up with old friends. Now, I have met a lot of dodgers in my time, having been concerned with the supply of Class A drugs for many years in Aberdeen and having worked alongside gangsters from places like Liverpool, Glasgow and Manchester, but these guys could give any of them a run for their money.

They would come in on market day, their livestock having already been transported into pens awaiting auction, and almost immediately they'd make their way down to where we butchery boys worked. Off into the little back shop they would trundle and out would come the bottles of malt whisky and Navy rum. Glass after glass would be poured as they slowly gathered together, discussing their little business deals and, of course, their latest scams. I used to find these characters so very interesting; I don't know why, really, other than I just knew that they were all at it!

There was this one crofter in particular, who used to come in quite regularly, and he was like the Godfather in rubber boots. He was a giant of a man from the south mainland, who owned most of the land down that way, and he was held in very high regard amongst his contemporaries. I can still picture him standing there in the middle of this little room, a tumblerful of whisky in his hand, with everyone gathered around him.

"You will never have money ...!" he bellowed out, while looking menacingly around the room. He always liked to make eye contact with everyone while giving a word of wisdom; he also liked to be heard!

A dozen or so men were crammed into our little back shop, the air blue with pipe and tobacco smoke, standing silently with their glasses poised at their lips, patiently waiting for this revelation.

"Unless ..." he shouted, before adding, almost in a whisper "... you have gone bankrupt at least twice and had about four good fires!"

The place erupted with laughter as they all lifted their tumblers, the contents of some spilling out over the edges and onto the sawdust below. But the thing was, on that occasion, at least, he was being absolutely serious. One of his barns had mysteriously burned down only weeks before, resulting in a massive insurance claim.

Being young and impressionable, as I undoubtedly was at that time, I was completely taken with the whole drinking thing and before I knew it I, too, was drinking far too much. There was hardly a night went by when I didn't go home from there at least a little under the influence, perhaps not steaming drunk exactly – although there were times when I was – but certainly never very far from it.

I then started going to the nearest bar during my one-hour lunch breaks, much to Brian's annoyance. Normally we would meet at my mum's house, which was always empty during the daytime, and get stoned on a couple of cannabis joints while watching that new phenomenon, *Neighbours*, on the telly, but alcohol soon became my number one drug of choice; it simply took over everything, although ever so subtly, and there, I suppose, began the great affair.

* * *

Sitting in the dentist's waiting area on that June day in 2008, with the form filled out in front of me, I proudly ticked "No" for smoking and answered "None" for the units of alcohol.

But there was still that question about hep C ...

Well, that afternoon I was finally able to tick the "No" box with all honesty and peace of mind. I would assume that most people reading this would also tick the "No" box, and think no more about it, but if you are like me and have had hep C, you'll maybe understand why it was such a big deal. You see, it was only the day before that I'd received the news I'd been hoping to hear, that the six-month post-treatment blood test revealed that I was still clear. Having already had two previous tests, which had both come back negative – one was a mid-treatment check and one was three months later when the treatment was finally over – I'd been waiting on this, the final one. Now that it was also clear, I was at last officially hep C free.

Almost seven months had passed since I had finished the combination therapy treatment for hep C, which consisted of two different drugs: interferon alpha, which had to be injected once a week, and ribaviron, which was taken orally twice a day over a six-month period.

Hep C, or the thought of it, had played such a big part in my life for so long that I wasn't sure how to react to the news that I was clear. Yes, I was pleased, but at the same time I wasn't exactly over the moon about it. Maybe I had become so used to the idea that it didn't really matter anymore, or maybe I had, in some strange way, enjoyed the whole experience. As is quite often the case with me, I never really understand the seriousness of a situation until it's too late, and even then I perhaps glean some form of satisfaction from it. Had my struggle with hep C been the same? I wasn't quite sure. It had certainly influenced a lot of my decisions over the years and, more often than not, the wrong ones.

But, sitting there that afternoon, I wasn't one hundred per cent sure about any of it. Yes, I was pleased that I had finally overcome my addictions and that my life – my body, even – had been restored, but at the same time, it somehow left this great big, dirty-looking question mark hanging over my head! I mean, how did it all go so terribly wrong in the first place and why did it have to be me? Did I really deserve to feel the freedom I now had, and what should I do with it now that I had it? Should I celebrate the success of the treatment, when I had undoubtedly left such a trail of devastation behind me, the extent of which I could have no real concept of?

Throughout my life I had hurt so many people and I wasn't sure how I should deal with that. I was well aware that alcohol and drugs had destroyed my life and I also knew that, as a result, my actions had ruined the lives of countless others – but why?

Sitting there in the quiet of that room made me think about the things I had done and the kind of person that was required to do them. So, how did I go from being this carefree 16-year-old, who enjoyed a little drink after his work, to becoming an alcoholic, drug-dealing drug addict?

Yes, what indeed had happened?

CHAPTER 2

I can remember like it was yesterday when my descent into the world of drugs really began. During the summer of 1983, when I would have been around 14 – 15 years old, I was given my first-ever smoke of cannabis. Of course, this was just my first real taste of *illegal* drugs; I'd already been using alcohol on a regular basis, as well as sniffing glue with a bunch of skinheads every other night of the week. However, cannabis, I quickly realised, was in a different league altogether.

Yes, it was the fact that it was illegal that held the biggest fascination for me. The secrecy, the risk – it was all simply far too exciting to not give it a go! My affair with drugs was quite simply something like this: I enjoyed the high, I liked the ritual of constructing a joint, but most of all I liked the danger involved and how this made me look in the eyes of those around me, whether disapproving or otherwise.

My walk with drugs during those early years was to take many twists and turns along the way, but I wouldn't have said there was ever really a definitive pattern to any of it. I mean, it wasn't as if I deliberately set out to become either one thing or another. "Beer head" and "druggie" were the two most common classifications around the town I grew up in, and I certainly wasn't either of those. I just didn't take any of it that seriously. Drugs and alcohol, to my mind, were simply something to experiment with; a curiosity, perhaps; a lot of fun, definitely, but that was really all there was to it.

I was by no means alone in this thinking. Just about everyone I knew was at it, some more than others, and as for "addiction", well, that was the last thing on anyone's mind.

As a group we were always more than willing to use anything that came our way: cannabis, amphetamine, LSD – if it was available, we used it.

I remember meeting a North Sea fisherman in a bar in Lerwick one Saturday afternoon. He was trying to sell a box containing around 50 ampoules of morphine. He explained that it'd been part of the boat's on-board medical supplies and because it was out of date it had been earmarked for destruction. Well, I didn't know much about morphine at the time, although I was fairly sure that it wouldn't matter if it was a little out of date or not, and so I bought the lot for something like £50.

The thing was, I had absolutely no idea what to do with them! I suppose what I should have done was inject them, but I was only 18 years old and dead against anything to do with needles. So, along with one of my equally-impressionable friends, I tried to smoke it, which certainly made for an interesting weekend, I seem to recall.

Regardless of whether or not I knew what to do with the morphine, the point I am trying to make is this: I just *had* to have it! It had simply been far too cool an opportunity to let pass me by. Such was my interest in drugs. An "inquisitive nature" coupled with a certain degree of "the need to impress" make for a deadly combination.

I can look back on those early days with a lot of fondness. They were a laugh – most of the time – and nothing too drastic ever happened to anyone, but having said that, we certainly didn't have the opportunities that young people in Shetland have today. Heroin, for instance, was virtually unheard of, except for a very select few; cocaine was extremely rare, and as far as I was concerned, a waste of good money anyway; and what was acceptable to me, as well as affordable, wasn't always that easy to obtain.

As frustrating as that often proved to be, we all found it very exciting, as you do when you're young, stupid and have nothing better to do, and whenever any opportunities presented themselves, whatever they might be, we quite literally jumped at them.

There was one particular incident that I think epitomises our keenness to experiment with drugs in those early days. It was a Saturday night in mid-September, 1983. A few of us had gathered in the shed in my back garden – me, Brian, and this other lad, Billy.

The garden shed, which was only ever used by me, had been kitted out with a bed, a sofa, a stereo and even a television set. It was like a second home. I would spend a lot of time there, either on my own or with some friends, smoking fags, drinking beer, perhaps playing my guitar. It also came in very handy whenever I had a girlfriend, or for occasions such as I'm about to describe ...

The three of us had been sitting around for most of the afternoon drinking beer, listening to music and just chilling out, when Brian suddenly had this idea that we should try "magic mushrooms".

Now, none of us had ever done "mushies" before, or anything of that nature. We hadn't long discovered cannabis and before that the closest thing to drugs we'd ever done – certainly speaking for myself – was glue sniffing, so this was very much uncharted territory.

However, after a bit of a discussion on the subject, as we weighed up the pros and cons of venturing into the unknown, we eventually set forth in the direction of the Staney Hill.

It was a drizzly, clammy sort of evening and by seven o'clock it was already growing quite dark. It certainly wasn't the kind of night to be wandering around on the top of a hill completely exposed to the elements, searching through the grass and heather for an elusive form of fungi. It was also one of those nights when those damned midges (small mosquito-like creatures that plague the hills and marshlands of Scotland) were constantly biting at your face, neck and hands as if they hadn't seen food before.

About ten minutes passed before a triumphant Brian bellowed out the good news that he had found some mushrooms. Having been at the golf course all week during his school lunch breaks helping some of the older boys to gather them, he thankfully knew exactly which ones to pick.

Billy and I ran briskly over to have a look, as neither of us was sure what we were supposed to be searching for. Brian stood there, his hand stretched out before him, and splayed across his palm were half a dozen or so rather scrawny-looking mushrooms.

"What? *That's* what we've to look for? Are you sure those are them?" Billy asked, nervously.

Billy just didn't like the look of them and now that we had found some, he was trying his hardest to put us off; at least that was the impression he gave. But Brian was not to be deterred.

"Yep, that's them all right. You can kind of tell because of that little nipple bit on the top. See?" he said, pointing his finger at what did, indeed, look a little bit like a nipple.

And so, without any further delay, and with no more excuses from Billy, off we all went in search of more.

Almost an hour of foraging must have passed when Brian finally announced time out. We gathered down by an old bomb shelter, a remnant from WW11, and emptied out our pockets.

"We must have hundreds!" Billy exclaimed, as we stood there, our hands cupped before us, filled to the brim. "Do you think that's going to be enough, though?" he asked, his tune having somewhat changed.

We stood there looking at one another.

"Well, I suppose there's only one way to find out," Brian answered.

Back in the warmth of the shed once more, we spread the mushrooms out on album covers to try to help them dry. Black Sabbath and Led Zeppelin were almost buried out of sight, as was the Who's "Meaty, Beaty, Big and Bouncy", which left poor old Pete Townsend and crew completely lost behind a veil of vegetation.

We then devised this really cool system, a bit like a factory line, where we would do some further processing. After all, none of us wanted to eat the wrong thing. Brian would pick out foreign bodies like grass, heather and any other less savoury objects he happened to come across, such as sheep droppings, and then set them in a pile before me. I then took off the stems and separated them into two bundles – heads in one pile, stems in another – while at the same time chucking out any that had those little white maggots crawling through them. Billy, who had an empty, plastic ice cream box, would then take about ten heads at a time and dry them off a little (as Brian had supposedly been instructed to do), with the help of an old hair dryer that I'd managed to procure from the house.

We all worked away quietly, drinking the odd mouthful of beer and slowly sorting through them until our patience began to run out. We then decided to eat the heads and only dry the stems, and when the stems were dry we would roll them up and smoke them!

"This just better be bloody worth it!" was all Billy could say, gagging on a few of those wet, slimy, little mushies, as they made their way slowly down his throat.

Close Encounters of the Third Kind was just about to begin on the television, so we stopped the music and decided to sit back and watch it for a while, and see what – if anything – happened.

We ate away at the heads and smoked the stems, until eventually they were all finished, and then we just sort of sat there, our faces glued to the screen, no one really saying anything, until Billy piped up: "This is a really good film, isn't it?"

Brian and I turned to look at him and burst out laughing! He looked so different. His eyes were wide and gleaming, his grin was half way around his head, his lips were quivering as if he was talking really fast and, as if that wasn't enough, I had this incredible feeling of butterflies in my stomach, like I was being tickled from the inside out!

The three of us sat there laughing almost uncontrollably at the most stupid things, and this went on and on and on for what must have been hours, until all of a sudden the lights went out and we were plunged into darkness!

That was the only problem with the shed, the power could be turned off from inside the house. It also meant that my parents had returned home from the pub, had probably had a little party and were going off to bed, meaning that it was sometime in the early hours of Sunday morning.

We sat there in absolute darkness – darkness like I'd never experienced before. It was almost as if it were alive. I could see flashes of green and red, and I began to make out little shapes darting around here and there. I then became very conscious of the fact that we were all three of us in this darkness together, and a feeling of paranoia began to take hold of me.

Trying to be really quiet, I listened out for the others breathing, just so I could get a grasp of what they were up to, but they must have been doing the same thing, for not only was it black dark, it was completely silent. The shed had been plunged headfirst into the twilight zone and I don't think any of us had a clue what was going on.

At least an hour must have passed and nobody had said a word, when out of nowhere, Brian's voice shattered the silence, causing us all to think.

"Do you think we should maybe leave the shed?" he asked, very quietly.

"Ahm ... Ahm no moving!" Billy said.

"Where about is the door?" Brian asked, timidly.

"I think it must be over there somewhere," I answered.

"Go and open it then!" Brian ordered.

"No," I said.

"Why not?" he asked, suspiciously.

"Just ... Just because!" I asserted.

"Well, I don't think anybody should move!" Billy recommended.

"Why not?" Brian and I exclaimed, in perfect unison.

And that was how it went for about the next four hours, until a very welcome sign that it was daylight began to appear around the edges of the door.

Our mushroom experience – although somewhat frightening to end up with – never put us off, with many a session, some good, some bad, in the years that followed.

* * *

Shetland and drugs – what is it about this place? Well, I suppose it's probably nothing new. I am sure the Picts, the first people to settle in these islands, had their little indulgences, especially with "magic" mushrooms being so readily available. Then, of course, there came the Vikings and it's unlikely they were unaware of their properties. Yes, I'm fairly sure they would all have had their "close encounter" moments, too!

I suppose the unfortunate thing for me was that I took to the whole drug and alcohol thing like a duck takes to water, but at the same time, it was hardly surprising. When you grow up in a culture where having a good time always involves the consumption of alcohol, then not only does having a good time become dependent on alcohol, it just readily becomes the accepted thing to do in most, if not all, of life's circumstances. If you happen to feel a little down or depressed, perhaps, a little bit bored or fed up even, then alcohol quickly becomes the thing to reach out for.

Now, I really don't mean to give Shetlanders a hard time here, but I do think it's important that we don't just view this as being particularly normal. This attitude to drink – consuming vast amounts of alcohol at any given opportunity – stems largely from a lack of maturity, from a lack of confidence, definitely, and has become something that we, as a people, are greatly dependent upon. Certain people will argue this point, I'm sure, but I doubt any of them can honestly deny the fact that Shetlanders are renowned for this mind-set the length and breadth of the nation. It is actually something a lot of islanders are extremely proud of, to the point of boasting about it regularly.

The unfortunate thing is that Shetlanders are also fast acquiring a similar name for drugs. As I write this, Shetland has been recognised as one of the worst hit areas in Scotland for heroin. That dubious honour used to belong to some of the small fishing towns along the north east coast of mainland Scotland, like Fraserburgh, but not so much anymore.

So where has this come from? What makes Shetlanders so susceptible to addiction? Why should heroin take such a hold so quickly? Well, I believe it has its roots in what we've been brought up to believe is acceptable behaviour.

When I was growing up in Lerwick, in the years leading up to the opening of the Sullom Voe oil terminal in 1975, everyone used to party, and there's nothing unusual in that. However, with the introduction of the oil industry, and the excess of money that was suddenly available, well, it all went a bit over the top.

Suddenly finding itself the centre of attention, no longer just an isolated scattering of rocks that most people south of Orkney wouldn't have given a second thought, Shetland had become, almost in the blink of an eye, a land of amazing opportunity. Sadly, this brought with it many negatives. All these strangers suddenly poured into the community from mainland Britain, introducing the locals to many different cultures, including drug culture. With an overabundance of ready cash at everyone's disposal, it was bound to have an adverse effect on a local population, who it has to be said were, in many respects, extremely naive.

Almost overnight, Lerwick was transformed from a mundane little fishing community to the Dallas of the North of Scotland. You would even see men and women strutting around town all dressed up with Stetsons and cowboy boots, as if they were off to a rodeo. It really was the weirdest thing, but that was how it was back then; everyone could suddenly afford it, and so everyone went that little bit further.

I can almost hear the cries of objection now. "So, what is so wrong with that? At least we never worked with those drugs!" (An expression I have heard on countless occasions.)

Well, yes, that may be true to some degree, but that depends on your definition of "drugs". When you consider the obvious harm that alcohol does, if it had only just been introduced into today's society it would undoubtedly be banned. It is one of the most destructive substances known to man, yet it is perfectly acceptable. In terms of addiction, what is the difference between being an alcoholic and a drug addict, anyway? Alcohol is legal – that is the only real difference I can think of.

I don't think it matters which part of Britain you come from, as everyone can probably relate to this to some degree, but the reason I believe substance misuse has had such an adverse effect on Shetland in the first place, is birthed in something rather innocent, perhaps rather romantic, and certainly respectable.

Shetland, ever since it was first occupied, and right up until they discovered masses of oil buried deep underneath the North Sea a few miles from its shore, has always been a very desolate, hard, almost unforgiving place to live. Those people who first settled here and tried to carve out an existence certainly never had it easy. With its barren, windswept landscape, the far-reaching, heather-clad hills and deathly sombre peat bogs, trying to scratch a living from it was, for many, quite literally a life or death situation. And if you weren't in a position to work the land, the only other alternative was the sea, where fishing was every bit as hard, and as the islands' history books will clearly tell you, every bit the widow maker, too.

Shetlanders certainly haven't had it easy. They have had to struggle to survive through every conceivable difficulty that living on such a dark, isolated, over-exposed scattering of rocks could possibly throw at you. So who could blame them for wanting to let their hair down when the opportunity arose?

Alcohol, therefore, has always been prevalent in Shetland's culture, simply accepted as an everyday fact of life, something to be revered, glorified even; but it is no longer just about alcohol, or magic mushrooms, or even a bit of weed, it is now heroin, crack cocaine, crystal meth; it is all manner of hard drugs, and with them come problems.

With the money came the acceptance of the "party all you want" lifestyle, but there also sneaked in a continual moving of the goalposts, and slowly, but surely, everything was eventually considered fair game.

* * *

My introduction to the bigger drug scene was exactly that; it was in the effortless moving of those goalposts. When taken into consideration along with everything else happening at the time, cannabis was seen as a rather harmless drug and was considered nothing much to worry about. What was so wrong with a bit of weed? It is, after all, just a plant, not too unlike the tobacco plant. Some people smoke it and it gets them a little high. So what? It's not as if they're harming anyone other than themselves. But is that really the case?

When you grow up with the attitude that it's okay to indulge – as long as you're having a good time and you're not harming anyone else – then it's highly likely you don't consider the effects that it may or may not be having on you or on those around you.

Like everyone I knew, I didn't consider any of that stuff. It was my life, my money and as far as I was concerned, it was my business and no one else's. Yes, it was my life and it was up to me what I did with it, and anyway, why should I listen to a society that prides itself on how much it can drink?

For some reason or other, I quickly went from being a "drug user" to a "drug dealer". No sooner was I using cannabis on a regular basis, at the age of 15 or 16, than I began dealing in the stuff. It just seemed to be a very natural path for me to take.

Looking back, I can now see how this seemingly harmless pastime escalated with the use of other drugs, like ecstasy and LSD, especially, I suppose, ecstasy, or "E", as it is more commonly known, mainly because of the social aspects associated with it.

When ecstasy first came onto the scene in 1988, or thereabouts, there was a big write-up about it on the front page of *The Sun* newspaper: "Ecstasy – the Love Drug Hits Britain". At the time of that article, I had a friend who was living in one of the major cities in England, where this new drug was supposedly circulating. No sooner had I read that newspaper headline than I received a call from him saying that he'd tried it.

"Peter! It's the best drug ever!" He'd shouted down the phone. "And there's no comedown, either!"

Within one week of that phone call, I received through the post Shetland's first-ever supply of "E"s, at the then princely sum of £25 per pill.

Ecstasy really changed me, as it did a lot of people I knew, and that was mainly because at that time, in drug terms, they were just so good!

The first ones I had sent to me were tiny green pills that looked rather unimpressive, to be honest. They were completely blank – certainly nothing like the ones you get nowadays with little motifs imprinted onto them – but they came with instructions for use: Bite in half, swallow, and whatever you do, do not throw up!

This, to me, was exciting!

I will never forget that night at The North Star disco in Lerwick. I was completely and utterly away with it. I had honestly never experienced a feeling quite like it and I loved every single minute – but from that night onwards something in me changed. I simply didn't want to go out unless I had one; clubbing just wasn't the same without it.

Needless to say, it wasn't long – maybe a year or two – before "E"s had found their way into every disco and nightclub in the country, but one thing I do know is this: none were ever as good as those first ones.

* * *

"Business" around that time picked up really fast and I was soon making hundreds of pounds each day, all from my parents' home. My mother and father were quite unsuspecting about this to begin with, but then it was nothing unusual for my bedroom to be full of people. Ever since I could remember, having no brothers or sisters of my own age, all the kids in our area seemed to converge on our house. I don't know why that should have been, but every day there would be a steady stream of kids coming and going from our place. You would think most parents would have become fed up with that, but it never seemed to bother mine. They were either very tolerant of all the racket, or they were just glad to have me where they knew I wasn't breaking the law.

By the time I was 16 or 17, things were going on in their house that they had no idea about. All these guys, who they'd basically watched growing up, were now streaming up and down our staircase, playing a whole new game – and getting completely wrecked.

Very quickly it all got out of hand. It was no longer just a little business on the side, but something rather more. The trips I was making south to Newcastle and London to obtain drugs were becoming ever riskier. The amount of drugs and the different varieties made it that little bit harder to traffic each time, adding to the pressure I soon found myself under. It was also around this time that rumours began circulating round the British Legion Social Club my parents frequented – rumours that I was a "druggie", and not only that, but a dealer, too.

This, of course, caused tension at home, with one confrontation after another. I flatly denied everything, even though it must have been plainly obvious to everyone what was going on, but that was just how it had to be dealt with.

My mother then took to searching my room on the odd occasion when I was out. I knew she was doing it, although she would deny it, but during one such search she found the evidence I had been so hotly denying.

There were times when I got so paranoid that I would hide my drugs in different rooms of the house, and one of these was a room she rented out to a lodger. On this particular day, she had obviously heard me going into that room and had put two and two together. I had then gone out to the pub and when I returned to fetch some of the cannabis, I found to my horror that the whole lot had vanished. Later that day I plucked up the courage to confront my mother about it. She admitted that she'd found it and not only that, she'd also found all the money – somewhere in the region of two thousand pounds.

It really came as a shock to her to find so much money and drugs, as she simply hadn't imagined the scale of it, but she then did something that really surprised me. She fetched the drugs and the money from wherever she had hidden them and gave it all back to me.

That did something to me that day – probably a lot more than if she had dumped it all – which wouldn't have surprised me, and to be honest, I wouldn't have blamed her if she had. But with that gesture something in me changed. I don't really know what that something was, I just know that it was then that I began to struggle with the kind of person I was becoming. All of a sudden I was no longer under the illusion that I was this clever guy, full of confidence, unstoppable even. No, I quickly realised that I was just some poor, misguided boy, who had completely lost the respect and trust of his two elderly parents, if I'd ever had it, and that was nothing to be proud of.

I left home at that point and went to live in a caravan up on the Staney Hill, in a brand new council initiative called Hoofields, a complete den of iniquity from the outset, but I didn't go there alone; something came with me – an overwhelming feeling of dissatisfaction. It was almost as if everything I had started to believe about myself had suddenly been washed out of me. I just did not feel good about myself – about anything, in fact – and I began drinking to excess and swallowing LSD, as if that somehow helped the situation.

Everything took a severe nosedive then. I started not caring about my wellbeing or the relationship with a girl I had been seeing for some time. My employment at da Marts, where I had worked for almost three years, had suffered to the point where I was forced to leave.

I just didn't want to do anything other than sit in the bar all day, deal drugs, drink vodka and trip out of my head on LSD. And all the while I would justify it to myself by believing that this was all I was good for.

CHAPTER 3

Things finally came to a head in the spring of 1990 with a much-expected raid by the local police. I had arrived back in Shetland the day prior to the raid, after an extended trip to Newcastle to buy drugs, with a strong feeling that something of that nature was imminent. In fact, the emotion was so strong that I'd anticipated being pulled by the police the moment I stepped off the overnight ferry from Aberdeen to Lerwick. And although that didn't quite happen – not that it would have mattered anyway, as I had sent the drugs on up ahead of me by general cargo – I still had this unshakeable feeling that something was going to happen.

So strong were those feelings that I made the decision that morning not to go anywhere near the caravan, even though there'd been no welcome party at the ferry terminal to drag me off to the station. Instead, I headed straight over to my girlfriend Fiona's home, which wasn't something I would normally have done. From there I was able to arrange for someone willing and trustworthy enough to collect the drugs from the P&O depot and bring them right to me.

Now, I don't know why I did the things that I did – or was about to do – but it was as almost as if I was being guided. Thinking back on it now, it was very strange how events unfolded; it was almost as if something – or Someone – was watching out for me.

With the drugs safely in my possession, it suddenly entered my mind, while still at Fiona's, that I should spend the night at my parent's house rather than at the caravan.

Not having lived at home for such a long time – or, for that matter, even visited – I just knew that I had to go there on this occasion. The problem I faced, however, was how to turn up at their door, after not having had any contact with them for so long, and avoid suspicion. Strangely, even that seemed to be sorted out for me.

My father had just returned home a day or so before after a spell in hospital. He hadn't been well for a while – not that I had seen much of him or known too much about it – but after being admitted to hospital for some tests a few weeks before, they had found it necessary to keep him in longer than predicted. This, then, provided me with the excuse I felt I needed to go to stay with them.

Later that afternoon I turned up at their door and, of course, with them being only too happy to see me, I requested a bed for the night. (It always made me feel a little guilty, the way they always welcomed me; it wasn't as if I kept in regular contact.)

I stuck my bag away in my old bedroom, and while doing that I listened again to that little voice: *Go and hide it somewhere safe*. And so, while they sat downstairs, I followed whatever was leading me and put it in what I hoped would be a suitably safe place.

After doing all I needed to do, I went downstairs to join them and the three of us sat in the living room while my mother and I chatted between ourselves, my father being a man of very few words. The conversation started off quite pleasantly, as usual, but it never took long before our little chat ended in an inquisition, which, I suppose, was the main reason I never went to visit them anymore.

"What are you doing to find work, then, Peter?" Mam would always ask. "Have you tried such and such, or have you thought about maybe doing this or doing that? Have you spoken with this company or been to see that company?"

And on it would go. My mother absolutely hated the fact that I was unemployed. She simply couldn't understand how anyone who was able to work wasn't working!

As soon as she had that out of her system, she would start on about another pet hate of hers, the rather more delicate subject of drink and drugs.

"Are you still drinking? Are you still taking that dirt?"

I would sit there, going through my usual routine of trying to reassure them that everything was all right and that there was absolutely nothing to worry about. Then, when it seemed she wasn't hearing me and was pushing the issue more and more, I would become defensive, which usually ended up with me getting angry and blurting out something that would cause her a fair bit of hurt.

"Look, would you just stop asking me these blooming questions! Stop hassling me, for gawd's sake. I came to see you, to see how you're doing, not to be flipping interrogated!"

And then, realising how hard I was being on her, without fail I would slip into denial mode, which usually meant lying through my teeth to make her feel better.

"Yes, I'm cutting down on the drinking" and "I'm hardly doing any drugs these days." I even elaborated on the supposed job search. "I've applied for this job and that job. I've contacted this person and that person. I'm actually doing really well at the moment," and so on.

But hardly a word of truth ever came out of my mouth anymore, and I think they both knew that. My parents certainly weren't stupid and I never, ever took them to be; it just seemed sometimes that the lies, as obvious as they might have been, were easier for them. I'm fairly sure there were times when they preferred that to the truth.

"Oh, well, that's good then," Mam would normally concede. "As long as you're doing something."

That particular visit was no different to what usually happened, except this time we had our dinner together, which was rare, indeed, and then at the first opportunity, off I went to the pub.

* * *

The following morning, at around 8 a.m., there came a bang on the front door. I heard my father's voice and then the rumble of heavy boots on the staircase, before they made their way across the landing to my room.

I lifted my throbbing, hung-over head from the pillow and looked at the bedroom door just as it swung open.

"Right, Peter ... Up you get!"

At least half a dozen police officers crammed themselves into that tiny bedroom and stood watching me rise naked out of bed. The man who'd shouted the command then began waving a warrant around in front of my face, as there, under the watchful gaze of everyone in that room, Fiona, who had stayed the night with me, and I began to dress.

After removing Fiona from their midst, they searched the room I was using, turning it almost inside out in the blink of an eye, but when they didn't find anything a decision was made to go against protocol and search some of the other rooms in the house, so sure were they that they'd find what they were looking for.

The truth of the matter is that there was plenty there for them to be satisfied with, their only problem was that they had no idea where it could be. They were up in the attic and out in the shed, they were up the stairs and down the stairs. All you could see were these little police bonnets going this way and that way, searching here and searching there, until eventually they gave up.

After about an hour or so, I was taken into the living room where my father and Fiona sat with a policewoman. I signed a form to say that they had been, that they had found some drug-related paraphernalia, like used "roaches" found under the edges of the carpet, gram weights from a set of scales – nothing of any real consequence – and off they all went.

I walked over to the window and saw them trundle, dejected, along the path, out through the gate and into their vehicles. But it really could have been so different. Standing there, watching them drive off, I knew I should have been going with them, but for some strange reason the one place that they never checked – and it was the one place that would have been the easiest to search – they completely ignored.

There was a wardrobe at the top of the staircase used to store linen and they walked past it at least half a dozen times, if not more, never once showing any signs of interest in it. If one of them had even bothered to open the door for a quick look inside, sitting on a shelf directly in front of them, covered only by a towel, they'd have found 1.5 kilos of cannabis resin and a few thousand LSD tabs.

Greatly relieved, I watched the cars pull away and with an almost celebratory punch into the air, turned to see my father, who had moved from the seat he had been kept sitting in, standing by the drinks cabinet. He was finally going back to work that morning, after having been off sick for about a month, and had been so looking forward to it. At that moment, however, he just stood there looking at me, his face a shade of grey I had never seen before. He was holding a bottle of whisky in one hand and a glass in the other and was shaking almost too much to drink from it, but he gulped it down when it reached his lips and just as quickly, that one was followed by another.

"Look, Dad, it must have been some sort of mistake!" I said, rather pathetically.

There was no reply. He just turned his back on me, set down the glass, pulled on his jacket and shuffled out of the house and down the path. I stood at the window and watched him walking up the road to his work, and I couldn't believe that I had allowed this to happen to him.

Somehow, amidst all of my drinking and drug carrying on, it had never really dawned on me that maybe I had hurt my father. All those years that we had lived together, I never really understood our relationship. He never got angry; he never shouted or swore; in fact, he pretty much never showed any emotion whatsoever.

But this time, as I watched him from the window, walking that lonely and painful-looking walk of his up the road to work, I knew that I had caused him a lot of heartache.

There had been something different in his eyes that morning, something I hadn't seen before. The way he looked at me just before he left the house ... It wasn't the raid, it wasn't even the drugs or the drinking, for that matter; it was something else. For the first time in my life I was seeing him as he really was. He had been greatly hurt, he was angry – and he'd finally had enough.

* * *

As far back as I can remember, my father, Peter Francis – or Frankie, as he was affectionately known – was never really a well man. He had a few physical ailments, the nature of which I am none too certain, and a chronic smoker's cough, of which I am.

Some people reading this might think this a poor way to begin describing my father, but the truth is it really affected me when I was growing up. My father just wasn't like other dads in our neighbourhood. Admittedly, he was much older than most, but he just wasn't able to do the things that they did. He was different from them in many ways, because of his physical condition, and this really saddened me.

You know, it truly breaks my heart to admit this now, but there were times when I was deeply ashamed of him, was highly embarrassed by him, even. In fact, there were times when I was really angry with him, although deep down inside, even from a very young age, I always understood that it wasn't his fault.

I think the problem for me was that I felt his obvious frailties, his lack of physical ability, his excruciatingly painful-sounding cough – which at times was so prominent in our household that when I had friends around would cause an uneasy silence – somehow defined me also. My father was weak, my father was ill; therefore, what did that make me?

Although it greatly affected me, I never once said an angry word to him about it and always tried my hardest to hide my disappointment whenever those feelings might arise. Yet, I couldn't help harbouring this deep resentment, which was very possibly expressed in other ways, hence the likelihood of me causing mischief.

It would also be fair to say that his health issues not only affected me and whatever opinions I may have formed about myself; they affected the whole atmosphere at home. I mean, it wasn't as if I was the only one who had a problem with it.

"If it wasn't for those bloody fags," my mother would often shout, a Benson & Hedges burning between her fingers, "your dad would be some fit man today!"

Yes, it was the cause of many an argument at home, although always very one sided and to me, extremely unfair. On many occasions this brought out of me a rather admirable show of devotion to my father. Laying aside whatever feelings I may have on the matter, I would instinctively jump to his defence, quite often finding myself in the middle of my parents.

"Maaam!" I would shout. "Just leave Dad alone. He can't help it. It's not his fault! Just leave him alone!"

I could never stand by and watch anyone giving my father a hard time, even if that someone was my mother – in fact, especially if it was my mother.

There was never any question in my mind how I felt about my father. I dearly loved him and was at times very protective of him, but it would also be fair to say that there was never any kind of real contact between us; there just always seemed to be this distance.

We lived in the same house and were always aware of one another's comings and goings. He would go his way and I would go mine, the two paths seldom ever crossing. Yet I suppose it was this strange kind of distance that made me love him all the more. In my eyes, he appeared to be a lonely person who was ignored half the time by those around him. Even in the midst of a roaring party he looked quite lost. He never seemed to want to speak up for himself either, especially when confronted by an irate wife, and he seemed unapproachable to a young boy who observed these things from afar and longed for them to be different.

As father and son, the one thing we never seemed to share was a proper relationship. A lot of people who knew him will probably read this and wonder how I can say such a thing, but the truth of the matter is that's just how it was or, at least, how I perceived it. And I'm not saying this to simply have a go at him or for any reason other than I think it is important. I certainly do not mean to be critical of him in a negative way, but merely examine what I feel is a very important part of my upbringing. The truth is, I never really knew my father in all our years of living together, until he lay dying on a hospital bed.

My father was just an extremely quiet, very laid-back man – perhaps too quiet and too laid back – but as a result there was just so much that we never did together or shared. He never joined me out playing in the garden or took an interest in whatever I might be doing; he never read me stories or told me tales about when he was young; in fact, as I write this, I find myself struggling to think of a single instance when we, as father and son, did anything together.

Besides his obvious health concerns and his lack of interest in me, my father was a very solitary man, which obviously didn't help matters. Strangely enough, some of my earliest memories are of me standing at the window of our council house, early in the morning before even the sun had risen, crying as he began his walk up the road to his employment at the woollen mill. There was just something about him, which even at such a young age, made me very concerned about him. He looked so vulnerable all of the time and I couldn't help but feel sorry for him.

That, I believe, was the crux of whatever bond we had. In my mind he seemed to struggle on through life, painfully, faithfully, every day the same, as I watched from a distance, silently, longingly, wishing things could be different. But there never was, and ever would be, any real kind of closeness between us, either emotional or physical. I don't remember him ever hugging me or holding me, and I certainly never heard him say that he loved me. But that was just how he was.

My mother, on the other hand, was the complete opposite of my father. She was a strong character and not just mentally, but physically, too. Having been brought up on a little working-class croft in the tiny village of Levenwick, the eldest of a family of eight brothers and sisters, she simply didn't stand for any nonsense. She was, without a doubt, the one in our household you had to watch out for, as she could certainly dish out a good hiding if and when the need arose. She was good with her hand, with a belt and on occasions, with whatever was handiest at the time.

My parents hadn't planned to have a third child so late in their lives. They already had my brother, Norman, who was 15, and my sister, Vera, who was 13. They had even suffered a miscarriage a few years after my sister was born, pledging then not to have any more children, but as their luck would have it, on August 4, 1967, they had me.

They were, in many respects, probably two of the nicest people you could ever hope to meet. They were well liked in the community and highly thought of in the British Legion Social Club, where they spent many an evening. Having me when they did obviously wasn't what they'd envisioned for that time of life, but they settled into it as best they could, while at the same time keeping up appearances, which was much more important to my mother than it was to my father.

I suppose the easy thing for me to say here would be that I was somehow neglected or starved of affection, but neither of those things can I honestly attribute to myself, certainly not through any deliberate act by my parents. But what I did do was bring upon myself this rather "unlovable" mantle. It seemed to me that nothing I did ever brought them any joy in life or made them laugh, and that was something I was to constantly struggle with. Then, of course, everything I did do, every decision I seemed to make, whether a trivial matter or something important, would be without fail the wrong one, and this, as far as I was concerned, was reflected in our relationship.

There was no closeness between us, no words of love were ever spoken, no hugs or kisses were ever exchanged. I felt constantly over looked, deliberately ignored even, and the more I understood about life – about my life – the more I believed that it was of my own making and all I deserved.

* * *

Ever since the day I could walk, I seemed to find myself in trouble. I suppose this came from the freedom I appeared to have. From earliest memory, I was pretty much left to my own devices. It was for this reason that things quite often fell on my sister, Vera, who I remember was there for me more than anyone else in a material sense and though she perhaps didn't realise it at the time, in an emotional sense, too.

Vera would have been in her mid to late teens during this stage in my life, and at first she enjoyed the novelty of having a little brother to look after – something she did rather well and which was much appreciated by me. At some point, the novelty began to wear a bit thin, especially when all her friends were going out and enjoying themselves. Sadly, through no fault of her own, there came a day when my sister couldn't be relied upon either, and I suddenly found I was more alone than ever.

Yes, as a child I had a tremendous amount of time to myself and with so much energy, I suppose falling in to trouble was somewhat inevitable. This tendency to cause trouble was a big disappointment to my parents, who simply couldn't understand it. They had never before encountered this kind of behaviour, when hardly two weeks would pass without at least one visit from the police.

While discussing this with my sister during the writing of this book, she told me a few stories, and one in particular has always stuck in her memory.

Vera had been standing in the kitchen, making something for us to eat, when there was a knock at the door. She stopped what she was doing and went to answer it, thinking it was probably a friend of mine, but instead she found a couple of policemen who had been sent to our address to "investigate a report of fighting between two groups of youths, in which stones had been hurled across a busy road, endangering cars and frightening pedestrians".

When they asked Vera if they could speak to "this Peter Jamieson" – the name they had been given of one of the main offenders – she recalled their shock when she took them to the back door and pointed out this skinny, little five-year-old boy, out playing with his toy diggers in his shorts and t-shirt.

No matter how often I was visited by them, I just never seemed to learn. In fact, the older I became, the worse I became. I don't really know why that should have been; I mean, I wasn't that bad a person. I never intentionally set out to misbehave; it just always seemed to end up that way. As I say, I loved my parents and would never have wanted to do anything to hurt them, but there was a definite streak in me that just couldn't be at peace, which often resulted in some catastrophe or other.

I know my father struggled to cope with my behaviour and my mother would remind me that this didn't help his health, but I couldn't seem to avoid it. No sooner would I have been given a good talking to by the police or a good hiding from my mother, with a reminder of how much I had disappointed my father, than I would be up to something else. It didn't seem to matter who I upset, what punishment I received, how sorry I was, or what good intentions I had thereafter, it always ended in some kind of nonsense.

Here's a very good example of this:

One lovely summer's morning, when I was perhaps seven or eight years old, I had been sent on a simple errand to buy in a few messages from our neighbourhood grocery shop. While standing at the counter asking for the various items my mother had requested, my eyes suddenly caught sight of those big, yellow boxes of Swan Vestas matches in amongst the cigarettes. I reached the end of the list and as the grocer stood there, hands on the counter, looking down on me with that big, friendly smile of his, almost without thinking I looked up at him and said, "and a box of Swan Vestas."

Without too much of an inquisition, I managed to purchase the matches and after dropping off the shopping, I called along at my friend Brian's. I can still see us standing there on his doorstep, me ever so proudly showing off this shiny, new box of matches – sliding them open, then closed, open, closed, open – and watching with amusement as his eyes grew that little bit wider with every glimpse. We then hurried off in the direction of the docks and quickly found ourselves aboard this old fishing boat, the *Research LK62*, which had been lying there for years, filling with water and slowly breaking up with every tide that came and went.

Now, I can't quite recall whose idea it was, probably Brian's, but it was decided that we would light a small fire in the corner of the wheelhouse. However, with it being an old boat and the wood being really quite dry, it started to burn faster than either of us had anticipated. And then, instead of trying to control it, if only to avoid drawing attention to ourselves, we got completely carried away and began adding anything to it that would help it burn, until the entire wheelhouse was ablaze.

Jumping from the boat onto the old, dry stone pier, we stood there in complete awe, our mouths hanging open as the flames leapt out through the broken window panes. Rising higher and higher, closely followed by a billow of black smoke, it began towering upwards into the blue summer sky, until all of a sudden ... The sound of sirens!

Running away as fast as we could, we hid ourselves behind some old, corrugated iron sheds and watched from a safe distance as a fire engine eventually arrived, followed by one of those very familiar "jam sandwich" police cars.

Deciding it was best not to stick around for too long, we made a commando-style escape through the sheds until we found ourselves in the middle of a caravan park. With black smoke rising up behind us, we began trying the doors of one or two of the more run-down caravans until we found one that wasn't locked and quickly hid inside.

The caravan itself was absolutely filthy; there wasn't a clean dish to be found. Every pot and pan had been used and left dirty in the sink and there was rubbish lying all over the floor, including empty beer cans, empty whisky bottles and playing cards with pornographic pictures on them. We hunted around for anything of any value or particular use, spent a little while educating ourselves with what those cards were about, and then piled some stuff in the centre of the caravan and set it on fire.

We then made our escape once more and ran across the northbound main road, hiding in one of the long-abandoned fish huts once used to house those people who moved from place to place following the herring fleets. From there we watched as flames engulfed the caravan and the emergency services were quickly redirected to yet another major fire.

While Brian sat at the window watching this Saturday morning mêlée unfolding, I disappeared for a look in some of the other rooms. Realising I had been gone for some time, Brian came looking for me, only to find – this time to his horror – that I had done the inevitable and set the room on fire. Standing there in the doorway, his mouth hanging open, he looked at me in utter disbelief.

"Peter! What the hell are you playing at?" he shouted.

We quickly exited the building and ran as fast as we could the 1,000 yards or so down the road to my house, grabbed an apple each, some crisps, a bottle of Hay's fizzy lime juice and made for an ideal viewpoint high up on the Staney Hill, where we could safely sit overlooking the scene below while having ourselves a little picnic.

It looked absolutely amazing from the side of the hill. Three plumes of smoke rose high up into the windless, summer sky, twisting and turning, obviously visible from miles around. Three separate fires, two fire engines, and at least two police cars, one of which we noticed leaving the scene of the third fire and making its way down the Old North Road, turning at the foot of North Lochside. And because we lost sight of it, due to the row of houses, we knew that it had more than likely stopped in the middle, somewhere in the region of number six.

"We are going to be in so much trouble, Peter!" Brian said, while munching on a mouthful of Smokey Bacon crisps.

And me? Well, I seem to remember not really having any feelings about it one way or the other.

* * *

At many stages throughout my childhood, my parents were at a complete loss what to do with me, but that decision was nearly taken out of their hands with visits to the Children's Panel, especially following one particular event. It was a couple of years after the fire incident, when I was about 11 years old and had been identified as being part of a gang that had robbed an electrical store in Lerwick. What my mother said then affected me more than anything else.

"This will bloody kill your father!" Mam shouted, as she read the letter summoning me to appear before the panel.

I remember her setting it down on her lap then looking at me scathingly, tears in her eyes, and saying something that really shocked me.

"Peter, can you not see what you're doing to your father? It's because of you that he is so grey headed. It is *your* fault, Peter! *It's your fault that your father is so ill!*"

Those words stung me to the very core of my heart. I absolutely adored my father. I was his protector, his knight in shining armour! How could they possibly think that I would deliberately want to harm him? It had never crossed my mind that I had been the cause of his ill health. I mean, he had *always* been ill, so how could it possibly have been *my* fault? But it somehow made sense to me and what's more, I believed what she said.

What I learned that day certainly made me think long and hard about the things I was doing, but it also made me extremely angry, because they had no idea about me. They simply hadn't a clue about the stuff I thought about, the problems I had and the hurt I felt because I was always such a letdown to them. And there was other stuff, too, stuff they couldn't have known; stuff, which for these very reasons I felt could never be disclosed.

The last thing I would ever have wanted to do was hurt my father and they should have known that – but how could they? It wasn't as if we ever talked. I only ever received their proper attention when I had done something wrong.

Yes, what I learned that day, and in the weeks that followed, was a defining point in my life. The realisation of what I was doing to my father, coupled with the threat of being sent to a "home for troublesome children", was the wakeup call I, perhaps, needed. And, yes, I suppose it did have a certain degree of success; it definitely made me calm down a little, or at least it made me more careful not to get caught. However, what it seemed to achieve more than anything was to further instil within me this belief that I was purely bad to the bone, an unwanted burden on society and on my two elderly parents and – worst of all – the cause of my father's illnesses, and these were beliefs that never left me.

* * *

Following the police raid in 1990, and the obvious damage it had done to whatever relationship I had with my parents, I made a decision that would hopefully protect them from any further hurt. I would move to Aberdeen, where they wouldn't have to see me or hear about me, and there I could pursue whatever it was I wanted to do with my life.

CHAPTER 4

When I first moved to Aberdeen a few months after the raid on my parent's home, it was with the idea of starting over and hopefully – by learning from my mistakes – avoiding the same pitfalls as before. Having worked in the drug scene for quite some time, I considered myself to have a good enough grasp of what was required. And surely in a relatively large city, which Aberdeen undoubtedly was – especially to someone from a place the size of Lerwick, with a population of 8,000 – I could "work" without too much of a problem. I had various friends who lived there, knew the city quite well, and had a few thousand pounds to work with. I also had established drugs contacts in London, as well as one or two in Newcastle, so what could possibly go wrong? The answer to that question was ... plenty!

Shortly after arriving in Aberdeen, I was joined by my girlfriend, Fiona. A few years my junior, Fiona was a very beautiful, young woman, with many inspiring qualities. She was clever, quick-witted and unlike me, extremely level headed. We had been together for almost three years, although somewhat on and off.

Admittedly, Fiona had put up with a lot. I was constantly messing her about, was always drinking and using drugs to excess, and during our time together I had fathered a son with someone else. But throughout it all, taking each problem as it came, Fiona was somehow able to forgive me and work through those difficulties, regardless of how they must have made her feel. The way I behaved in our relationship was inexcusable, but deep down in my heart, and as unbelievable as this next statement might seem, I cared for her tremendously. So, why, why all this chaos in what could have been a wonderful relationship?

Well, I just seemed to have a nagging feeling that life wasn't going to be too good for me in the future. I could visualise myself growing into this gaunt and soul-less figure, becoming ill in my later years and slowly disappearing into insignificance, which wasn't something I was particularly looking forward to. In fact, it was a realisation that drove me to utter despair.

My actions towards Fiona, towards myself, towards life in general, were symptoms of an overwhelming sense of hopelessness. I mean, what was I to do when that time finally came? If I thought so little of myself now, how was I going to feel about myself in the future? And what about Fiona? That was the big issue. Could I really put her through all that? I was, at times, very confused – afraid even – and I think subconsciously I hoped to avoid whatever lay ahead by slowly destroying it all before it came to pass.

Before long we had set up a flat together and Fiona managed to find work in a cocktail bar. I, of course, had no intention of working and instead took to the bars of Aberdeen, where I hoped to ply my wares.

To begin with everything seemed to work out fine. Every day I was meeting up with more and more people to sell drugs to and business began to develop, but it didn't take long for that all to change. Soon I found myself with a decision to make, which in the end wasn't too difficult.

Constantly treading on other people's toes was always going to have its consequences and so, after a couple of tricky situations and a few bruises to my body, as well as my pride, it became plainly obvious that the best – and certainly the healthiest – thing for me to do, was give it up. Finally, after a run of perhaps six months I, too, found myself working full-time in a busy, city centre bar.

For the remainder of that first year, life in Aberdeen probably wasn't too bad for us; we were both in full-time employment and Fiona was even looking into the possibility of doing a long-term college course. After what had been a rocky beginning, with a few disappointments thrown in, things finally settled down and life became quite normal.

But there, I think, is where the problem really lay. It seemed that in no time at all, when everything appeared to be going so well for us, I started to become a little fidgety, in need of some excitement, perhaps. Gradually, through trial and error, I began finding ways to satisfy that need.

I started dealing small amounts of drugs to some of the bar staff, and then to some of the customers. I discovered ways to fleece money from the till and would even think up elaborate schemes to smuggle alcohol off the premises, and whenever the opportunity arose I would help set up the odd drug deal for people coming down from Shetland. Without realising what was happening, I found myself once again entrenched – trapped, perhaps – in that same old vein of dishonesty.

It was also around that time that I first acknowledged I was suffering with some form of depression. I had never before put my actions down to depression or used it as an excuse for behaving the way I did, but I remember becoming very aware of how much it affected me.

Subtle to begin with, the feeling slowly began to intensify, filling me more and more each day with this sense of hopelessness. *What's the point of it all?* I would often question, and the answer was always the same. *There isn't one.* I then found myself becoming emotional, perpetually swinging from one extreme to the other, happy one minute and sad the next. I could wake in the morning full of the joys of life and within minutes hate myself and wish I were dead. But what bothered me more than anything was that I suddenly found myself doing exactly what my father did; I struggled on, silently, never saying a word to anyone, which added considerably to my woes.

So, was it then just a coincidence that I began dabbling with heroin? Not that it was a cause of the depression, but was this perhaps a reason why I began using it in the first place? Was it, perhaps, a means to an end, as they say?

* * *

Heroin was a drug I always swore I would never use – its destructive nature was the basis for that decision – but ultimately it was that same destructive power that drew me in. For a little over two years of living in Aberdeen, surrounded by all kinds of drugs, as well as opportunities to use, I had managed to stay away from it, but that all changed.

To begin with, Fiona was quite unaware that I was using heroin. It took a few weeks before she finally found out and when she did nothing much was made of it. What must have seemed like "a little here and a little there" was hardly going to worry her, not having any experience of it herself, but then I don't suppose either of us realised just how much a little every now and then could become.

A few months into it, that perception quickly began to change, as it struck me how detached it made me and how uncaring I was becoming. Eventually I began to feel a little guilty about what I was doing – guilt not being something I handled very well – but that wasn't before Fiona revealed just how fed up she had become with the relationship itself.

I came home one night, a mixture of high on heroin and a little drunk, to an almighty argument that resulted in Fiona being quite hurt. I remember standing looking at her, the tears streaming down her face, disgusted with myself at how I could hurt her so, and then realising that I simply hadn't been doing right by her for quite some time; in fact, I hadn't been doing right by a lot of things.

Fiona was a lovely person, great fun, hardworking and honest, and all that she ever really asked of me was that I cared and wanted to spend time with her. But I was always too engrossed in myself and what I was doing to even notice what effect it might be having on her – until I saw her standing there before me, her heart completely broken, and it dawned on me just how utterly selfish I had become.

I had completely stopped caring about her, about her needs as a person, as my fiancée, even. Somewhere along the line, I seemed to have lost all regard for her and our relationship – which had been obvious for some time to Fiona – and it hurt her deeply.

So, I made a decision there and then to try to change, at least enough to bring a little comfort back into her life and hopefully see a smile once more on that lovely face of hers. She just looked so fed up and I could hardly blame her, but more than that, she also looked extremely vulnerable and that was something I could not allow to happen. If nothing else, I would not be guilty of neglect.

Within a week or two of that argument, as well as being accused by the management of stealing from my employers, I gave up my job behind the bar and tried hard to cut down my alcohol consumption, which I considered my biggest problem. I also vowed to give up my little indulgence of heroin, although I was surprised at how difficult that was, considering the relatively short space of time and infrequency of usage, and I promised myself to cosy up once more with Fiona.

Life then took a positive step forward. I had a renewed hope for our relationship, for myself even, and began to view things differently. I found work in the butchery department of a superstore and decided that I didn't need to sell drugs anymore. We began looking for another flat in which to make a new start, and I even gave up the odd night playing guitar in a band, as well as nights out playing for a pub darts team. That's how serious it all became!

However, as always seemed to be the trouble with me, I would take really drastic measures when circumstances hit a low and then, when life got tough or became too dull, I would eventually find myself back where I once was, and quite often worse than I was before it happened.

Without going into any more detail about this, let me just say that it didn't really matter what I tried to do, because it never lasted. When the cosiness of home became stifling, and the man inside hadn't changed – as if he ever really would – resentment broke free, all reason was lost and I was back tooting on heroin and drinking heavier than ever.

It was shortly after this that Fiona's sister, who had been living with us, found some foil I had been using to smoke heroin rolled up and stuffed behind a pipe in the bathroom. An almighty confrontation ensued and though I managed to somehow convince everyone that I had only been using it on the odd occasion, I felt so ashamed! I then became extremely defensive and tried justifying the heroin use by telling myself I was no good and this was all I deserved – a life of addiction and depression. Quite pathetic really.

If I am completely truthful, my motives for doing what I did next can be found in the above statement. I just wanted to think of myself as someone who had suffered in life, someone who had been so hurt and rejected by those who should have loved him that he'd been reduced to this pitiful state of addiction. Well, that certainly made life a lot easier. It made it easier for me to hurt Fiona, it made it easier for me to break off the engagement, it made it easier to just accept the awfulness of what I was about to put her – *us* – through, as I then turned my back on her, the flat, everything we had, and walked out of the door for the last time. And I did so with only one thought in mind – to see where this road would lead me. Fiona stayed on a while longer to finish her college course and then headed back to Shetland alone.

After dossing around for a week or two, I found a room to rent in the Torry district of Aberdeen and it was then I began dabbling with syringes. The first time I used a needle was about two weeks after breaking off with Fiona, and I only ever did it really because of that broken-hearted feeling. If ever anything in the history of mankind is a perfect example of a poor excuse, it has to be self-pity. I simply relinquished the purity of my blood because I felt sorry for myself.

There I was, sitting in a flat in Mastrick, an area of Aberdeen, feeling like the world was against me, and inwardly fighting this self-imposed loneliness by violating my veins – yet another thing I always swore I'd never do –

by injecting. From that day on, though not every day, I used heroin intravenously, and this went on for at least nine or ten months, a blatant contradiction of my ethics once more.

I had made a complete mess of my life and I wasn't particularly bothered where it was all going to end. Whatever values I may have held were quickly vanishing, but I would never forgive myself for what I did to Fiona; it was something that would haunt me for years to come.

But, life carried on.

* * *

Alcohol was most definitely my thing – I simply couldn't go a day without it – but all of a sudden I found that my needs also included heroin, which at the time suited me just fine. Although I perhaps didn't require it in the same way I needed alcohol, it quickly began to occupy its own space.

My heroin usage wasn't every day, as I somehow kept it manageable. I suppose I became what you might call a "pay cheque junkie". I would binge when I was paid, but as my money began to run out, which didn't take long, considering the demands the Child Support Agency was making on me, I would always make sure I had enough for a drink, even if only a few pints when I finished work.

It's strange thinking back on it all now, but there were a number of people who admired the way I did things back then and to be honest, that didn't really help matters. I know that what they saw was this completely reckless guy, who didn't have a care in the world and took massive risks with his health in his pursuit of drug utopia. To them it was all quite fascinating and I can understand why, but the truth was, I was actually very lonely and really quite depressed. I honestly didn't want to be a part of life any more, and quite often what they took to be exuberant behaviour was quite simply the out workings of someone who really didn't want to live. Thankfully, I never had the courage at that time to do anything about it, although it crossed my mind on countless occasions.

I suppose this made what happened next seem all the more peculiar. It came as something of a shock to everyone – including me – when I suddenly got engaged to a woman called Kareen, and very soon after that, married! Who would ever have thought that in the midst of all that mayhem anyone would have taken me seriously enough to want to be with me, let alone marry me!

It was some eight to nine months after Fiona and I split up that I began seeing this girl I worked with in the butchery department. We had been fairly good friends for a while, going out to the pub together on occasions, growing quite close, and then one thing eventually led to another. At that time Kareen already had a partner, who worked and lived abroad, but she chose instead to be with me.

Kareen knew exactly what I was like and what she was letting herself in for. She knew that I used heroin, although perhaps not that I injected or how much I used and, of course, she knew I liked a good drink. She also knew that I was planning to stop the heroin, if and when we became a couple, which we eventually did. With the aid of alcohol, I then managed to cope without heroin.

It was a struggle for a few months, with plenty of nights out, but it seemed to work. The whole marriage thing, however, took us both a bit by surprise, as we were too busy getting drunk every day to really consider what we were doing. In fact, the idea of marrying had sprung up one night after yet another drunken argument, and once our families became involved, that was it.

It all happened so fast; we got on really well when we went out drinking and before either of us knew what was going on, we were tying the knot in this lovely, little country chapel in a tiny, picturesque village near Montrose.

The whole business, romantic as it sounds, was doomed from the very beginning; in fact, it didn't even last a year.

Going out all the time drinking was one thing, but trying to live together as husband and wife ... Well, that was something else entirely. The marriage quickly disintegrated, as did my employment at the butchery department, and I suddenly found myself separated, homeless and unemployed.

Perhaps what happened next was inevitable. I received a bumper pay-off cheque from my employers and quickly set up in business once more. Having made an abundance of contacts over the years, this was relatively easy to do. I loaded myself up every night with ecstasy, and whatever else I could sell, and descended yet again on the bars and nightclubs of the city centre. It was where I longed to be and all I wanted to do, but no sooner was I making a good go of it – and thoroughly enjoying myself – than I met a woman named Tracy, and through her I began dabbling in heroin again.

Weeks of unadulterated mayhem were quickly followed by a steady decline back into the dreamlike warmth of heroin and to be honest, I never batted an eyelid at any of it. This, after all, was where I belonged. It was what made most sense to me – until I received a wake-up call that turned everything on its head.

We were at an address in the Rosemount area of Aberdeen, just across from the Bullring flats at the Viaduct, where we'd gone to score some gear. I was in the process of preparing a hit when this girl came walking into the middle of the room and crashed down into a seat across from me. She was going through some heavy withdrawals and began asking everyone for any used filters. (Addicts will normally save up their filters to use again later.)

Out of everyone that was there, only one person offered to give her theirs and I couldn't help noticing that it came out of a spoon, which had already been shared by about three people.

She rubbed her nose and thanked them. "Aww, cheers, min," she said, in a typical Aberdonian accent.

At that point I began to feel really sorry for this girl, begging for used filters amongst a group of people who couldn't have cared less about her, and who didn't even like her, by the reaction of some. I also couldn't help but be drawn to how pretty she was – or would have been, had her face not been so ravaged by the lifestyle she undoubtedly led. This touched something in my heart and so I offered her my filter and, in the same instance, gave her the tiniest bit of solution from my syringe. I warned her it had already been used but, of course, that didn't matter.

She crouched down on her knees at the table and began working away quite happily with what she had been given, making it ready in her spoon, until a few seconds later, just as she was about to administer the hit, her boyfriend walked into the room – at least, I think that's who he was. As their eyes met, a look of surprise appeared on both their faces, and almost immediately, after a quick look over the table, sussing out exactly what was going on, he lunged towards her and more or less ripped the needle out of her vein.

She let out a painful cry and began whining.

"'At wis fir me, Brian, 'at wis fir me! PJ gave me 'at, nae you." She sobbed bitterly. "PJ, tell him 'at wis fir me. Wis it, PJ? PJ, *tell* him!"

I could only watch in horror, unable to even open my mouth, as I had never witnessed anything quite like it. He shoved her away, gave me a sideways glance which clearly said "don't even think about it, mate", then sat down with his back to her and began to roll up his trouser leg in search of a receptive vein. It was, without a doubt, one of the most depressing things I had ever seen, making me question this whole carry-on, and what my part in it was.

What are you doing with these people, Peter? Just look at them! It's time to do yourself a favour and sort your head out.

And then, all of a sudden, as I looked around the room at the state of some of the individuals I was rubbing shoulders with and worse, a disturbing thought crossed my mind.

Peter, forget what this asshole has done, and think about this for a minute ... How many spoons have you *shared?*

Four different people had contributed to that one pathetic hit, I realised, four different blood sources – five, if you included hers – although they had certainly shared before. And then an even worse thought came to mind.

How many needles have you shared, Peter?

My mouth went dry, the effect of the hit all but disappearing, as I realised the answer to that question. Some!

I looked at Tracey sitting next me, slouching over with the effects of a hit, and a cold sweat began to form on my brow, as all those little ailments I'd been suffering over the past few weeks, like headaches, nausea and colds, began to make perfect sense to me.

That's it, Peter, you've done it now, boy! You're full o' the AIDS!

I simply couldn't take being in that room any longer. I immediately stood up, ignoring the argument that was gathering momentum, in which my name was being thrown about, and left never to return to that address again.

The following afternoon I was good to my word and I made an appointment at a clinic. A week or two later, on April 10, 1997, I was placed on a methadone reduction programme, under the direction of the Drug Problem Service (DPS), Royal Cornhill Hospital. But it was a complete nonsense from the very beginning and in as little as three months, I was chucking it all in and planning a return to Shetland.

* * *

The programme, as far as I was concerned, hadn't been going at all well. In fact, I was on my second or third final warning by the time I decided to leave. It just hadn't been working for me and it seemed an utter nonsense replacing one addiction for another, when it wasn't even the heroin that was the main problem, but my attitude towards life.

Completely and utterly fed up with it all, I called my doctor and told him how I was feeling and what I was planning to do. However, he was having none of it, and immediately wanted to arrange for me to receive my methadone in Shetland. But I was thoroughly sick of the stuff and had absolutely no intention of taking methadone ever again, and I pretty much told him that.

I had a different game plan – although it was a mystery to me exactly what that was – but sticking around Aberdeen on a methadone programme that wasn't doing me any good certainly wasn't what I wanted to do with my life. I needed to get off the stuff and away from everyone around me, especially this woman who I had to share my methadone with on occasion, and as annoyed as the doctor may have been about this decision, I had to get out of Aberdeen.

A quick call home to my mother, an exaggerated story of woe, and a seat was booked on the next ferry back home to Shetland.

Once at home, having met with everyone, I finally felt able to relax, something I hadn't been able to do for months. Fair enough, I had to undergo the usual third degree question time with my mother, but once that was out of the way, everything seemed very peaceful.

Of course, there was a serious side to my being there, which couldn't be ignored. The last seven years in Aberdeen had quite simply been a disaster, with a string of failed relationships – including two engagements and a marriage – trips back and forth to see various doctors about my drinking and drug taking habits, and periods of homelessness and unemployment. Now, here I was, returning to the family home at the end of it all, hooked on methadone, with who knew what diseases flowing around in my bloodstream. My life simply needed to change and that's what I hoped to achieve.

Now, anyone who knows Shetland and understands how things work here would agree that wouldn't be easy, not with all the drinking and drug taking that goes on. However, such was my predicament that I truly didn't know what else I could do. I had a comfortable, warm room there to sleep in, people who cared about me and genuinely wanted to help, and I didn't know anyone to score from, or even if heroin was available. It was, as far as I was concerned, my safest bet if I genuinely wanted to clean up my act.

But Shetland can be full of surprises, and this trip home was to prove no different, with one particular incident that really made me think.

* * *

I had been home for almost two weeks, had rattled (had withdrawal symptoms) on and off between bottles of vodka and the occasional use of recreational drugs, such as cannabis, and I was most definitely on the mend. Even my parents had relaxed considerably. So, although the fortnight hadn't gone by without incident, things were going much better than any of us had anticipated. A lot of that success had to be put down to the help of a few old friends who supported me – more than the effort being put in at home – and one in particular, Alastair.

The hardest thing for me to deal with was the lack of having something to do, as things could go a little haywire when I had too much time to think. I was, therefore, very thankful for those who understood my dilemma and tried to alleviate these situations by making time for me.

As I sat alone at home one day – I had no money, and my parents had refused me another handout – Alastair called along, quite out of the blue, and invited me out that afternoon. He was going to play a couple of rounds of golf and thought I might like to go with him – not to play golf, as that wasn't something I was interested in, but to do a little trout fishing at a loch right next to the course. Having spent many a day, or weekend even, fishing for trout when I was young, I gladly accepted his offer.

It was a beautiful, sunny afternoon and Asta Loch looked so peaceful. I found myself a good spot at the north end of the loch, cast out my two lines and lay back on the grassy bank, eagerly watching my bubble floats gently bobbing on the silvery, still waters. With a warm summer breeze blowing on my face and a can of lager in my hand, it was blissful. I was chuffed with myself for finding the energy to go, and also for the opportunity to have a drink, courtesy of Alastair, who supplied me with half a dozen cans of lager.

Every now and then my floats would disappear beneath the surface and just as quickly pop up again. I would reel them in, knowing that the worm had more than likely been taken off the hook, and so replace it and cast it back out again. That really was all the action I was having that afternoon, but disappointing as this was, it didn't bother me too much. I was just happy to be where I was and doing what I was doing.

A good hour and a half had gone by when Alastair appeared at the top of the grassy bank where I was sitting, shouting that he and his friend had decided to play another round. He hoped I was all right with that, which I was. The sun was still shining, the waters of the loch looked as beautiful as when I first arrived, and I still had three cans of lager to drink, so all was perfectly well with me – except that I was beginning to run out of worms.

I waved Alastair goodbye and opened the jar, knowing there couldn't be many left, and there in the bottom were two of the scrawniest worms you ever saw. I picked myself up from the grass, set down my lager and decided to go on a mission around the side of the loch to see if I could find some more.

Stone after stone after stone I lifted, working my way slowly along the grassy verge, but to no avail; there were simply no worms to be found anywhere! What was I to do? I had almost reached the end of the loch and looking back at where I'd been, I decided I had gone far enough. I began walking back, looking for other stones to lift, but those that were left seemed far too big to move – apart from possibly one. I took a moment or two to size it up and then, out of pure frustration and nothing more, decided I would try to lift it.

After a bit of a struggle, I managed to get it up on its end and when it was at an angle where I could balance it with one hand, I looked beneath it. And right there before my eyes, in all its wormly splendour, was the biggest, fattest, juiciest worm I had ever seen! Immediately, I bent down to pick it up before it had a chance to slip away, but just as my fingers were a mere hair's breadth away from touching it, it curled up into a tight ball.

This gave me a bit of a fright, to be honest, and I wasn't sure what to do for the best, but I decided that because it had taken such a massive effort to find it, it would go in the jar with the rest. If the need arose, I would decide whether or not to try sticking it on a hook.

At least another hour went by before I decided that it was time once again for the changing of the worms. I reeled in my lines, took off what was left of my nibbled-at bait, and opened up the jar. What I saw next completely dumbfounded me. There was now only *one* worm left in the jar – the big, juicy worm that could turn into a ball at the merest of touches.

I closed the lid and sat down. Had I been seeing things? Had there really been three worms in that jar to start with?

Just then, Alastair and his friend appeared, having finished their golf.

"Any luck?" he asked.

"No," I said, and then told him what had happened concerning the worms.

Alastair immediately threw down his clubs, slid down the grassy bank, picked up the jar and opened it. We both looked in and to my horror the worm (almost six inches long, purple-ish brown, flattened, sticky, glistening and pointed at both ends) seemed to be climbing up the inside of the jar, somehow using its mouth and its other end – whatever that was – to cling to the sides as it made its way to the top.

Alastair, being the brave man that he is, tipped it out onto the palm of his hand, and immediately the same thing happened as before; it curled itself up into a tight ball.

"See, I told you! That's the exact same move it made with me!" I said.

We watched it for a while, until eventually it began to unravel itself.

"Do you know what that is?" Alastair asked, the words spitting from his mouth with a certain degree of disgust.

I studied it with a bit more depth, but still only seeing a worm I didn't answer him, for fear of being wrong.

"That's one of those damned New Zealand flatworms, PJ!" he exclaimed. "People buy these plants that have been imported from New Zealand and the idiots take them outside and plant them in their gardens, as if they were somehow supposed to be here, and these little buggers came with them and now they're eating all our worms!"

He then broke it in half and squeezed out its innards between his forefingers.

"Bloody cannibals!" he said.

I didn't know much about flatworms, but I did know, as Alastair turned that poor thing inside out, that there was a lesson in this for me somewhere! From the outside it had looked just like any old worm, then it had acted like some kind of freak, and shortly after encountering some humans it didn't look like much of anything, just a pile of mush in the palm of Alastair's hand.

* * *

Anyway, fishing story aside for a moment ... Having come off the methadone, I managed to get through those couple of weeks living at home with my parents, and with relative ease, too, I must add – although it wasn't all plain sailing. I was constantly tapping money, coming home totally smashed just about every night, and never showing any real sign of caring about my predicament. But all in all, it wasn't as bad as it might have been, and my parents handled it very well. They were used to seeing me in various states of drunkenness, so it wasn't as if that ever came as a shock to them, but perhaps what did bother them was my uncaring attitude to whatever lay ahead.

My father had worked hard all his life, from when he was a young boy helping to run a small village shop, until he'd had to give up work rather early in life due to ill health. My mother, the eldest of eight children, definitely knew what hard work was, too. Yes, they were more than aware how tough life could be, but not when the troubles you had were avoidable and purely of your own making.

Heroin, for instance, what was all that about? Sticking needles into your arms – where was the sense in that? As my mother quite often pointed out to me, "There are people starving to death in this world, children dying every day of malnutrition, while healthy young people simply choose to throw their lives away because they can't be bothered!"

It was a life wasted, as far as they were concerned, and that was where their sympathy ended. They had long since given up trying to lecture me about how I lived my life, and I knew fine well what they thought of it.

Within the space of three weeks, I had reached a place where I felt strong enough to leave home again. I had achieved what I had set out to do, in the sense that I had avoided methadone and heroin during that time, and then it was time to go, a conclusion, I think, reached by us all.

My mother, hoping that this time things might be different, handed me a sum of cash, which I immediately counted and mentally began turning into drugs.

What makes me so cold-hearted? What kind of a person does this? I remember thinking, as I stuffed the money into my pocket and headed out of the door, giving her little more than a farewell nod as I closed the gate behind me. But that was just how my mind worked, no matter what I had been through, or who I might hurt.

I thought about this again later that night, as I sat once more on the ferry back to Aberdeen. *What kind of person have I become? Surely I wasn't born to be like this?* I pondered my existence and the possibility that it maybe wasn't real, that it was, perhaps, a dream or something.

Then my thoughts drifted off to that worm at the side of the loch. How did it get there? Why did I have to be the one to find it? That poor thing had travelled thousands of miles from New Zealand to end up in Shetland, only to be snatched from the ground by some strung-out idiot who stuck it in a jar and ... Well, you know how it ends. But did something like that need to happen to me, too?

My life, up to that point, had been fraught with mishap; in fact, there never seemed to be any let up to the misery that followed me, so what was the solution? Perhaps I, too, needed to go on a journey. Maybe I needed to get lost, or maybe I just needed to be found. Or perhaps what I really needed was to have my innards squeezed out of me!

Whatever it was I needed, it would have to be drastic or I was never going to change, that much was obvious.

CHAPTER 5

Cocaine. Okay, that's probably going to be the shortest sentence I write in this book, but let me tell you, it is completely loaded! If I were to record every event of any interest on this subject, I doubt there would be enough memory on my computer to hold it all. The things that I have seen and done as a result of that stuff, most people would probably never understand, but let me just say this: I have never encountered such craziness in all my life.

Now, it's not my intention to go into too much detail, but I would like to enlighten you on a few little matters that I feel are very important to my story.

You see, cocaine wasn't a drug that I was ever interested in before January 1999, but from then on it completely dominated my life, until I found myself lying in the back of an ambulance being rushed into hospital after a failed suicide attempt in April 2006. So what took place during that time for it all to end so dramatically?

After returning to Aberdeen from Shetland in August 1997, having successfully beaten the methadone, I tried my best to live as normal a life as I possibly could. Not wanting to rush back into full-time employment, I enrolled instead onto a college course, and was very quickly booted off – which didn't really come as any great surprise. Also, around that time I found myself in a relationship with a young woman who wasn't into drugs!

Within a few weeks of partying mostly, we moved in together, and after a relatively short period of unemployment, I began working for an offshore supplies company down on the harbour.

From mid-November '97 through to September '98, I was like a completely different person. I was much happier than I had been, was without a doubt far healthier, and for once in my life I was a lot more focused on what I was doing – at least, that's what I thought. I was still drinking quite heavily whenever the opportunity arose and dabbling a little with drugs, although mostly at the weekends, which was a vast improvement on previous years. Yes, I must admit I felt very good about myself. It was the most together I had been in a very long time.

In the autumn of 1998, however, perhaps a year after Sonja and I moved in together, all that began to change. My father, who had been sent to a hospital in Aberdeen to have some tests, was diagnosed with prostate cancer and the decision was quickly taken not to operate. As far as the specialists were concerned it was too far gone, and my father was nowhere near strong enough to undergo a procedure that had little chance of success.

Coming as something of a shock to the rest of the family, my mother especially, their only solace lay in the care that he would receive. This, along with the right medication, would offer him a reasonably comfortable quality of life for the time he had left, without going through the trauma of cancer treatments. It was a decision that ultimately only my father could make, but it was strongly advised by those who knew best, and as usual it was accepted by him with no fuss whatsoever.

Regardless of how this news was perceived back home, I seemed to take it really quite badly. I'm not too sure why, but almost immediately Sonja, who was a foreign student and perhaps as much as ten years younger than I was, began to notice worrying changes in me. It began with me not going home straight after work, choosing instead to sit in a bar. Then, after a while, I wasn't returning home until late at night and more often than not I was in a state: extremely drunk, wasted on drugs and on a few occasions with blood running down my face from a fight.

This didn't go down well with Sonja, as it wasn't something she was used to, but her feelings on this were seldom ever taken into consideration. Yet, she struggled on, hoping that everything would eventually calm down, but as much as I respected her for hanging in there, at times even sympathising with her, they didn't. And so, by December of that year, after what I can only describe as a depressing few months, we were verging on breaking up. In January 1999, she moved out for good.

With nothing to stand in my way, I packed in my job down on the docks – admittedly under increasing pressure from my employers, who were becoming fed up with me not turning up for work – and decided to try my hand once more at drug dealing.

Turning my days into nights, flitting around various bars and nightclubs, I resumed my career by dishing out ecstasy tablets – which always promised a quick turnover of cash – and quite successfully, I must add. But as time passed, and the more people I met in with, it became increasingly obvious that I needed to be selling something different: cocaine. It seemed that almost everywhere I went everyone was after it.

However, it wasn't until I happened along this rather strange, little Pakistani fellow, Fieder, that I was able to source my first regular supply. Somewhere in his late forties, Fieder wasn't the kind of person I would have expected to be living this lifestyle, and to be honest, he wasn't the kind of person I would normally have taken to either. He was brash and a little too loud at times, but he had exactly what I was looking for.

Without knowing anything about him, Fieder could easily come across as this colourful, friendly character, who would never do you wrong, but beneath his sometimes flamboyant and extremely charismatic exterior, there lay a shadowy side to old Fieder; he was very clever, incredibly cunning and although he might appear innocent to the uninitiated, he was constantly at it, 24/7.

Yes, from the moment Fieder entered the bar you could almost see, in those sharp, dark as pitch, smiling eyes of his, that devious little mind going into ultra-scam mode, where absolutely everyone and everything became a potential business opportunity. It really had to be admired, especially in a bar as hardened as The Pond was reputed to be. It certainly wasn't something you learned overnight, but Fieder had it down to a very fine art.

Laying aside whatever prejudices I may have held about this man – the fact that I simply didn't trust the man being the most obvious – our paths began to cross more regularly, and gradually Fieder and I became better acquainted. I had some decent money at my disposal, which he was very interested in, and he had some useful contacts, which made this connection between us somewhat inevitable.

Our relationship quickly developed and became a partnership/friendship that suited us both. Fieder, shrewd as he was, soon had me running around Aberdeen trying to shift 10-kilo packs of cannabis resin, and in return I received cheaper deals on the ecstasy and cocaine, which ultimately was what this was all about. It was, at times, hard work, there's no question about that, and Fieder could be extremely demanding, as well as a real pain in the neck. However, it was also quite good fun, and on rare occasions reasonably profitable, too, but more than anything, it was essential to my overall plans.

Ultimately, what I sought from this relationship, and the reason for putting myself through what was quite often a heck of a lot of hassle, was the prospect of it leading to bigger and better things. But this meant somehow getting beyond Fieder and meeting with those nearer the top of the ladder, who in this case were a couple of gangsters from Liverpool named Itchy and Scratchy. After all, 10-kilo packs of cannabis resin were not easily dispersed.

Now, it was plain from the beginning that Fieder had absolutely no intention of setting up a meeting between them and me, which in fairness to him I could quite understand; Fieder was onto a nice little earner. But the matter was soon taken out of his hands. Itchy and Scratchy, who made regular trips north of the border to collect their paper (money), didn't particularly trust Fieder, and on discovering that someone in Aberdeen, who they'd never met, owed them somewhere in the region £16k, they wanted it delivered in person. I admit I was a little nervous at the call when it eventually came, but it was exactly what I had been working towards and, therefore, extremely satisfying.

I began dealing direct with Itchy and Scratchy from that point on, much to Fieder's annoyance. We became better acquainted each time we met, although I never did feel at ease with either of them, even when things were going well between us. They were just very different from what I had experienced in the past, and I was never quite sure where I stood with them.

Anyway, I was off to a flying start with my new-found bosses; in fact, I very quickly became their number one choice in Aberdeen.

"How much does that kid want?" they would boast. "Make sure you give PJ whatever he asks you for," was a common command given to whoever was dropping off supplies. Fieder could only scratch his head as I went from strength to strength in their eyes.

"Where in Europe does that kid want to live?" they would often goad him, as the money kept pouring in.

Yes, for a while it must have looked as if that kid from the North could do no wrong.

Aha ...!

* * *

By June that year my father lay in a hospital bed, dying of cancer, and I was more than a little fortunate to have the opportunity to spend some time with him before he passed away. But before I left Aberdeen to make my way back to Shetland to my father's bedside, I had to make a quick decision about what to do with my so-called business.

There were a lot of drugs that needed to be sold and a lot of money to be made, but due to a few week-long binges – something I was prone to – I was lagging well behind with both. A quick calculation of cash and stock revealed a personal shortfall of about £4,000, mostly through my personal consumption of cocaine and alcohol, which wasn't very good from a business point of view.

And so, rightly or wrongly, not really knowing how long I might be in Shetland or, for that matter, when Itchy and Scratchy might show up for their paper, I made the decision to leave everything in the hands of my sidekick, Palsy, who would hopefully bring in some much-needed cash while I was away.

Palsy was an old school friend who'd moved to Aberdeen with his girlfriend, perhaps a year before. He had met in with me and was quickly drawn into what I was doing. His relationship with his girlfriend eventually ended as a result, and he came on board full-time. Palsy knew this line of work only too well having plied his trade, like me, in the bars and clubs of Lerwick; it should have been a formality for him.

Unfortunately, the decision to leave Palsy in charge turned out to be the wrong one. By the time I returned to Aberdeen a week or so later, my business had all but collapsed, with Palsy landing me in what appeared to be, after a quick calculation, an additional £2,000 worth of debt. Palsy had, for want of a better description, completely lost the plot. With access to so much money, and whatever else was available to him, it had all gone to his head. He was eating out in fancy restaurants, ordering expensive meals and bottles of wine from the menu; he was spending all day going back and forth to the bookies, instead of doing what I'd asked him to do, namely, sell drugs. To top it all, he'd been inviting these lap-dancing friends of ours back to our flat, a three-bedroomed squat, and holding wild parties.

Yes, Palsy knew how to live all right, especially when it was with someone else's money, which I fully appreciated. However, there was a major problem with what he'd been doing in that it wasn't *my* money he was squandering. If it had just been mine, then that would have been easily dealt with, but it wasn't. It was Itchy's money, and Itchy didn't like Palsy, which made things very awkward for me.

I remember sitting there that morning as he explained how much money he possibly owed me, and how sorry he appeared as he realised just how much trouble I could be in as a result. I had little to say about it, one way or the other. I suppose I could have completely blown my top, punched his face in, perhaps, but I didn't. In fact, it never even crossed my mind to be angry with him. If I remember correctly, after hearing his story and all he'd been up to in my absence, I actually laughed, which I think took us both by surprise, although it really shouldn't have.

You see, the crux of the problem wasn't what he'd done, how much he'd messed up, or even how much of my business he'd blown, because by that time I was already well up to my scrawny little neck in it. No, the real problem, I realised, was something else entirely, the nature of which only became apparent as a consequence of what Palsy had done. The fact was I really didn't care anymore.

There I was, sitting in a bar on Market Street, with Palsy looking at me through a haze of tobacco smoke, a large vodka in my hand, a couple of lines of cocaine numbing my system, my business hanging by a thread and an unworkable debt of somewhere between £4 – 6k to a couple of erratic gangsters, and the more I thought about it, the more I realised how little I actually cared. But where had this kind of reasoning come from?

I suppose I had been on a slippery slope since February or March, when I first began injecting the cocaine. I had stopped caring about myself – about life – almost to the point where what I did to myself at times might easily have been viewed as attempted suicide. I was putting together hits that were capable of killing someone and injecting them without any concern for myself. It was nothing at all for me to overdose at that time; in fact, it happened quite frequently, sometimes two or three times a day.

Needless to say, this carelessness, if that is all it was, brought with it countless problems, perhaps not so much for me – because I just didn't care anymore – but certainly for everyone around me. Palsy, for instance, found it extremely difficult. He liked a good carry on, the same as everyone else, and enjoyed the perks of what we did, but even he had his limits. Injecting wasn't his thing, and watching his best friend overdose probably wasn't much fun for him, but he respected what I chose to do.

The important things in life – health, money and friends – seemed to lose their significance. I just didn't see the point in caring about any of it anymore and subconsciously I think that is why I did what I did. In one sense it was quite easy, when it felt as if there was nothing left to live for – and when the people I owed the most money to were, for the majority of the time, hundreds of miles away in Liverpool.

Life was simply one scam after another. Every waking moment was spent trying my hardest to stay afloat, just so I could keep it all ticking over – even if only for another 24 hours – while constantly risking death. And it wasn't only the drug taking that was a danger to life. Continually playing off four or five separate suppliers against each other, just so I could keep it all going – while praying that none of them would catch me out – was extremely precarious. But when expenditure far exceeded profits – as mine did – and you weren't quite ready to give it all up, there was no other alternative. This was just how it had to be. It was, as they say, a do or die situation, the latter being the more likely outcome!

Regardless of Palsy's obvious mishap, I managed to pull it off for a while longer, fobbing off the different suppliers I grafted for with various scams and excuses, and admittedly thoroughly enjoying the challenges this often set me. But crunch time finally arrived at the beginning of August, when Itchy decided to call time out on all monies owed. He couldn't have picked a worse time for such an exercise, as I owed them somewhere in the region of £14k, and with only about £7k circulating, I was way off the mark.

When Itchy called that Friday morning to say he wanted all his paper in – something he had never requested before – Palsy and I both knew I was in a lot of trouble. The truth was I simply didn't have it and try as I might, I just couldn't figure out a way to swing it.

It was, therefore, no surprise two days later to find myself waking from a state of unconsciousness, lying naked in the bottom of a shower, being washed down of my own blood.

Injecting the cocaine definitely contributed to the trouble I landed myself in, and for that reason I think it would now be fair to introduce a man named Sykes.

* * *

Sykes was a past acquaintance of mine who after a chance reunion in a nightclub I discovered was doing the same thing as I was – running around for a bunch of gangsters from somewhere south of the border, supplying drugs in and around Aberdeen.

Having lost all contact with him for a few years – largely due to him having been sent to prison – it was a pleasant surprise to find out that after so long we were both still up to our old tricks. But no sooner were we reacquainted than I was back on the needle. Sykes, it transpired, was into shooting up the cocaine, and I soon began to dabble with it myself. Of course, I can't blame him for that happening, even though it was Sykes who first injected me with heroin some years before, but it was definitely his influence that led to the events that followed.

Realising our paths had taken such similar routes, we often met up. We shared our experiences, discussing those we dealt with, who owed us money, who was in for a hiding, that sort of thing, although we kept our work very much separate. I dealt for my group, he dealt for his; I had my graft and he had his, and that's the way it stayed. But so similar were our circumstances that it was good to compare notes, and we made a point of meeting up daily, generally after I'd finished conducting my day's business. We'd go somewhere to shoot up, usually back at the squat I shared with Palsy, and it was during one such meeting that Sykes first proposed robbing our suppliers and leaving the country.

Now, I didn't really know what to make of that to begin with. It was fun to fantasise about it, but that was it really, as far as I was concerned. It was interesting listening to his ideas about what he would do if we were to pull it off; however, it was about as realistic to me as landing on the moon.

Yet, as time passed, the more Sykes went on about it, the more I began to realise that he probably would go through with it, if the circumstances were right. And a little further down the line, when things started going wrong for me – Palsy's contribution being somewhat to blame – those discussions with Sykes became that bit more serious. All of a sudden the moon didn't look quite so far away.

By the end of July, I was hanging on by the skin of my teeth, owing money to just about every dealer in town. I had been threatened numerous times and had made countless enemies; I had been bundled into the back of a car on one occasion and threatened with having my arms broken. Another time I had been taken to a flat in Torry and made to sit in the middle of a room, surrounded by some rather serious-looking people, and threatened with much the same sort of thing. When I think back on it, and some of the situations I found myself in, I wonder how I managed to get away with it for so long, and with so little consequence.

But, then, I didn't get away with it for long with Itchy ...

* * *

Itchy finally called, summoning me to a meeting at which all debts needed to be cleared. Unfortunately for me, all I had to give him was a pittance of what I owed. In fact, I never went to the first meeting, as there was simply no point in handing over what little I had. They summoned me a second time, then a third time, until eventually, after being persuaded by Fieder and Rolf, a friend of his, I knew that it would be in my best interests to get it over with.

A little later, I walked into this room where Itchy and Scratchy sat on either end of a sofa. As I arrived, everyone else rather conveniently left, leaving the three of us alone. They then asked me to explain where their paper was and why I didn't have it all, strongly stipulating that it would be better for me to be honest.

There they sat, listening to my excuses, even looking sympathetic at times, dropping the odd comment like: "Oh, that is a real shame, PJ" and "Oh, poor, poor you" and so on, until they'd heard all I had to say on the matter.

Once they'd finished with their little game, I was made to stand in the middle of the room and strip to the waist. They sat looking at my skinny, needle-marked body, and then I don't remember anything.

Intravenous addicts were purely scum in their eyes and only ever tolerated if they served a purpose. An intravenous addict, who had been stringing them along, would normally be as good as dead. The only thing that saved me that night, I truly believe, was the fact that up until then they had genuinely liked me.

As soon as I regained consciousness in that shower – my eyebrow split open and hanging down across my eye making me half blind, with a puddle of blood swirling around my legs and down the plughole – I knew that it was time for Sykes' plan.

The following morning, I met Sykes and he had it all worked out. I was to break into the flat that was used by his supplier as a stash, go straight into the living room, jemmy open the two doors of a built-in wall unit, and take every holdall in sight. If everything went according to plan, when I arrived back at the lock up we would divvy up the loot and go our separate ways.

"That's all you have to do, PJ. It really will be as easy as that!" he said, grimacing at the state of my battered face.

The thing was, he had made it all sound so very simple, but standing there in the middle of that lock-up garage, with half my face taped up, I wasn't totally convinced. Nor, for that matter, did I particularly want to have to go through with it. On the other hand, what choice did I have? Itchy and Scratchy had certainly made their intentions quite clear, and a torn eyebrow, as well as a fractured cheek bone, were nothing compared to what potentially awaited me. I just had to hope that it was going to be that simple.

Later that morning, I did everything Sykes told me to. I watched from a distance as his suppliers left the block of flats, saw them pile into the cab that would take them to the bar where they always went for a drink at that time of the day, and then I moved in. All kitted up like a council worker, with overalls and a tool bag, within seconds I had breached the door of the ground-floor apartment and was into the living room, bursting open the doors of the locked unit, which contained all five holdalls: their entire stash of drugs, cash and – worryingly – ammunition.

Then, in as little as two trips, which took about five minutes in total, I had it all transferred into the boot of a car. In around 20 minutes, from start to finish, I was back at the lock up and it was all over! It had been that simple; in fact, it had been far simpler than either of us had imagined.

There were more drugs in those holdalls than I had ever seen before and certainly more cash than I had ever handled. The drugs had a combined value, I would guess, of somewhere in the region of £100k, with an additional £65k in cash. Not bad for 20 minutes' work! But that was only the beginning of it – the easy bit, shall we say – as all hell broke out across Aberdeen.

Reports were constantly coming through about people being hurt. There were rumours of fights breaking out between certain gangs, as the blame for what happened made its rounds. Sykes, who at this point was still going around with them pretending to help, would call me most days to keep me informed of all that was happening, and it didn't sound very nice. Possible suspects were taken out into the woods and threatened with shooters, and all sorts of things were happening to various people throughout the city. I just had to try hard not to think about it too much and carry on doing my thing – running around selling drugs and sticking needles in my arms – as if nothing had occurred.

But a lot did take place as a result of what we did, and it wasn't good. Several people were very seriously hurt, and some, as a consequence of some action or other, were even thrown into prison to serve rather long sentences. One guy in particular, whose stash it had been, received seven years, while another man, who had been innocent of the initial robbery, received eight years for his part in something related to the incident.

And me? Well, I kind of got away with it. And yet, I didn't really.

* * *

The day after the robbery, I attended a meeting with Itchy and Scratchy and paid them the £4k I'd been short. There were quizzical looks all around as I walked into that room, with the two of them sitting there on the sofa, eyeing me up and down, obviously checking out their handiwork as I strolled into their midst.

I simply threw their cash down on the table and it was clear that they didn't quite know what to make of me. This skinny, little drug addict from Shetland – who at one time could do no wrong and for a while was their star player – had turned out to have been stringing them along, making complete fools out of them to the extent that they'd beaten him unconscious. Now, here he was, two days later, walking straight in, as if nothing had ever happened, and throwing down their cash with a look in his eyes that asked what all the fuss was about.

Itchy just smiled and shook his head a little, grabbing the wad of notes from the table. And Scratchy? Well, he couldn't have cared less about the money, preferring instead to beat me up all over again. Thankfully, he was overruled.

Approximately two weeks later, Sykes was found out for his part in the robbery. They'd somehow figured out that he'd been involved and from that his suppliers had also found out about me. But rather than come and pick me off the street first, which would have been the wisest thing to do, they made the mistake of going for him.

You see, Sykes was a very clever guy and capable of a lot more than people gave him credit for. He certainly wasn't one to fall for some half-hatched plan.

First of all they took him for a night out on the town, as if they didn't suspect anything, and after having a good laugh together, even lavishing cocaine on him, they all headed to a flat somewhere for a drink. Along the way, Sykes had a distinct feeling that all wasn't as it should be, and he decided at the last moment to go home instead. Just as he turned to leave, a fight broke out. CS gas was sprayed into his eyes, and he was dragged – fighting against them as hard as he could – into the flat, where they proceeded to tie him up.

Thankfully, someone in the block of flats had either seen what had happened or heard his screams and called the emergency services. Shortly afterwards, the police arrived, burst in through the flat door and rescued poor Sykes from whatever was in store for him. He was then taken directly to hospital as the rest of the gang were arrested.

Two days later, I met up with a frightened and battered Sykes. He told me in great detail what had happened leading up to the events in the flat, and what they knew about us. He was also able to tell me what was going on with them in custody, and that they were due to be released the following morning. How he knew all that, he never said, although I had a good idea, but according to Sykes something would have to be done, and quickly, or we were both finished.

The following day I was sitting in The Pond, thinking about the mess we were in, and all the drugs we now had to somehow get rid of, when my phone rang. I looked at the screen and saw it was Sykes. Rather hesitantly I answered it.

"Hey, PJ!" he shouted. "Wait till you hear this!"

Sykes then explained how they'd all been released from jail that morning and had gone straight to an address somewhere on the south side of the city, where they'd been swooped on for a second time.

I just sat there at the bar, looking at my partial reflection in a glass of vodka, feeling a real sense of hatred for everything I had become. I felt like a sewer rat, or something equally as undesirable. I also remember hating the very sound of Sykes' voice as he described how the Armed Response Unit, who'd been lying in wait for them, had gone bursting through the door. Sykes had also heard from this reliable source of his that they had been caught with cocaine worth thousands of pounds, as well as firearms.

Some hours later, the details of the raid were announced on the *Grampian News*. The whole of The Pond went quiet, as it always did when a local drugs bust was mentioned on television. I sat on my stool, trying hard not to look too interested, as people's attention was drawn to the screen in the hope of seeing some photos.

"A significant breakthrough in the long-running battle against the drug gangs of Aberdeen" was how the newsreader relayed the views from the Queen Street police station. This, they boasted, had been largely due to "information received from the public".

I had played a massive part in that so-called "breakthrough" – me and my utterly selfish needs, that is – and right away I realised I had completely overstepped the mark.

As far as Sykes was concerned, there was nothing now to worry about and that was effectively the end of the matter. In his mind, there was no one left with enough conviction or bravado to do anything more about it! Personally, I wasn't so sure, although I really had to hope that he was right.

* * *

Then the fun really began. I suddenly had more money and drugs than was good for me and had thousands upon thousands of pounds stashed at various addresses throughout the city. One or two of those places belonged to people I trusted, while one or two people were totally unaware that money and/or drugs were being hidden there. The drugs were by far the biggest problem – especially the 30 kilos of cannabis resin. They took a little longer to secrete, but after a while we managed to get it all stashed away quite comfortably.

What I did next was go totally over the top with party after party, nightclub after nightclub, and even the odd trip to the casino. What a mess I was fast becoming. I was pure skin and bone by this time, gaining the rather unflattering nickname "toast rack".

But that's cocaine for you; it has a habit of making you lose weight, whether you're eating enough or not, and at that time I could go days without eating anything. And not only did my physical health begin to really suffer, but my mental health did, too, as I began having some odd delusions.

For example, I started thinking of myself as some kind of machine. I remember having a hit in the toilets of a city centre bar, then putting the spoon back into my pocket and the lid back on the syringe. As the full force of the hit began, I opened the door of the cubicle and stepped outside. The electrifying rush of the cocaine was pulsing through my body and I stood there, taking long, deep breaths, while concentrating on my rapidly pounding heartbeat.

Just then, in the mirror in front of me, which was spread the whole length of the wall directly above the sinks, I saw myself standing in the middle of the room. For a moment I couldn't work out how it could be me. It was as if someone else was standing in my place, looking menacingly back at me, but I couldn't seem to avert my gaze. I was completely transfixed. A spotlight right above my head shone down, making my eye sockets look like empty, black holes; my face was sunken and skeletal, reminding me instantly of the cover of that Irving Welsh novel, *Train Spotting*.

I stood there, rooted to the spot, uttering words that made no sense, until the sound of music from the bar penetrated my mind, bringing me back to reality. But even that wasn't enough to wrench me from this nightmare vision, as I stood frozen, looking at myself in the mirror, one ear listening out for any one approaching the toilets.

Against the music in the background there was the constant *whoosh, whoosh, whoosh, whoosh* in my head, as the cocaine worked its way through me.

And then a thought suddenly occurred to me, almost as if someone had spoken it:

See, this is what you have become, PJ. This is what you have turned into. You are a machine, cold and heartless, and that's all you'll ever be.

I was, I knew, an empty shell, hollow and devoid of feelings, and as I stood there in the grip of this rush, with blood running down my arm and my head buzzing with that high-pitched whooshing sound, I smilingly embraced it.

"Yeah," I responded, and then began saying under my breath, in time with the almost engine-like "whooshing" that filled my head, "The machine ... The machine ... The machine", over and over again.

CHAPTER 6

One of the worst things about cocaine is undoubtedly the paranoia. If you're using it regularly enough, there is no way you can avoid it, no matter what you do, and it seems that the longer you use it, and certainly the more you use it, the worse the paranoia becomes.

Within approximately six months, I had reached a stage where absolutely everything I did was affected. The simple things in life seemed to suffer most, such as going into town on a bus, or popping out to the shop for a packet of cigarettes. It could be someone walking their dog past my window, or a stranger merely glancing at me from the other side of a busy street; it really didn't seem to matter what the circumstances were, as soon as the paranoia began, that was it. Everyone and everything – regardless of how simple, innocent or just plain ridiculous – became subject to this almost insane scrutiny, which at times was a cause of great embarrassment, and quite often financial loss.

Here's one instance that illustrates the point ...

I had been up all night/morning shooting up cocaine and drinking vodka, as was my usual. At around 10 a.m., I decided it would be a good idea to try to offload 1 oz. cocaine, which I'd been carrying around in my pocket for almost 24 hours.

Leaving the owner of the flat I was in sleeping soundly in their bedroom, I let myself out and headed towards the town centre. I'd hardly walked ten feet from the door when that feeling of paranoia began to hit; suddenly every car that drove past was the Drug Squad and anyone who even looked in my direction was an undercover officer – and, of course, they were all part of an elaborate plan to catch me out.

Realising I couldn't return to the flat, as the door had locked behind me, I turned left off Nellfield Place and onto Great Western Road, where I hoped to drop off the drugs at a friend's house. However, as soon as I turned the corner all I could see – especially in front of the house I intended to visit – were police and CID everywhere. I panicked, pulled up my hood and quickly spun around, deciding instead to try to lose myself in the busyness of a Saturday morning on Union Street, the commercial centre of the city.

Reaching the top of Holborn Street, I turned onto the shop-laden thoroughfare, unsure where I should go or what I should do. With people surrounding me, going in and out of the high street stores, I bobbed and weaved my way down through them, trying my best to outmanoeuvre my pursuers. I then began making sudden changes in direction, almost knocking people over at times, and even walking out in front of moving buses in a vain attempt to somehow lose my followers. But with cars slamming on brakes to let me cross, and even sounding their horns in annoyance, I knew I was only making matters worse – and yet, still I kept on.

It became fairly obvious that it was only a matter of time before "they" closed in on me, putting an end to this dangerous little game with the traffic, as every time I looked behind, I could see them drawing ever closer. I therefore decided to make straight for the harbour as fast as I could, where I would toss the cocaine into the sea. And so, once again I started to dodge and weave my way down through the shoppers on Union Street, until I reached the top of Market Street, where at last I could see my destination approximately ten minutes away.

But then another thought crossed my mind, as I began to doubt if they would allow me to reach it. So, being the sly, old fox that I was, I turned right at the bottom of the road onto Guild Street, and headed instead in the direction of the Criterion Bar.

Taking an opportunity to look behind me, I noticed that they, too, had turned the corner, very cleverly disguised as a group of middle-aged ladies out shopping. I then looked ahead and there they were again, coming at me from the opposite direction. This time they were camouflaged as a couple of oil rig workers, complete with off-shore bags. It then became imperative that I reach the door of the Criterion Bar before they worked out what my plans were. So, with my eyes fixed firmly on the entrance, I steamed on ahead, determined to make it.

With sweat pouring down my face, back and chest, I at last reached the door of the Criterion and quick as a flash ducked inside, hopefully fooling everyone. Once safely inside I ignored the waiting barman, walked straight to the toilets, into the cubicle, locked the door behind me and victoriously flushed the cocaine down the loo.

What an amazing feeling of relief when I opened the door and walked out of the toilets, ready at last to face my pursuers. Striding on past a suspicious barman, a flurry of snappy bags used to sell grams of cocaine dropping to the floor in my wake, I stepped out through the doors and into bright, glaring sunshine – where I fully expected to be busted – only to find myself all alone, with not a soul to be seen in either direction. My feeling of elation quickly turned to one of extreme sorrow.

Yes, just one story out of many.

I did discover later that there had, indeed, been a lot of CID and police activity on Great Western Road that morning, focusing on a tenement block of flats directly next door to the house I had planned to visit. A young woman had been found stabbed to death in what was described as a "frenzied knife attack" at the door of her apartment.

There was no question about it, those paranoia attacks caused me a lot of grief, but as tortuous as they quite often were, they weren't even the worst of it. There were many occasions, for instance, when the paranoia would hold me captive, sometimes for hours on end and often in a state of complete terror. Yes, there was many a time when my friends and I would find ourselves completely barricaded inside a house or flat, imagining all kinds of horrible things were waiting outside, planning to get us.

Certainly life was a little crazy, but if the cocaine wasn't enough on its own, everything really took off as a result of a crack cocaine epidemic that now swept through the streets and suburbs of Aberdeen. Gangs of "Yardies", as they are commonly known, had targeted the oil-rich city, and were flooding its streets with the cocaine based drug, which in no time at all completely turned the drug scene on its head. And I – being the kind of person I was – soon found myself very much in the thick of it.

My first recollection of crack was at a party somewhere. I was handed a crack rock – a pipe with which to smoke it – and fell in love with it almost immediately. Thereafter, come about 9 p.m., I would leave Palsy and Fieder in The Pond and sneak off up to a flat on Crown Street, where I would buy as much as I could afford. Then I'd go somewhere and smoke it, pipe after pipe, until it was all finished, regardless of how much of it I had bought.

It certainly wasn't a cheap affair. For instance, 0.3 g, which seemed to be the most common quantity, would cost £50, hence the reason it was commonly referred to as a "nifty". From there on, multiples reduced in price; for instance, a "teenth", which weighed roughly 1.6 g, would cost £180, and so on up to 1 oz., which could set you back £1,450 – an amount I bought once and smoked solidly for about four days. I became far too paranoid, and did too many strange things, to ever buy that quantity again, thankfully.

I remember trying to estimate just how much I was spending on crack during any given night of the week, and I discovered that it averaged between £180 and £250. Just how much this new habit was costing me was obvious, but still I carried on, having somehow managed to convince myself that it was actually doing me some good.

You see, up until then I had been injecting somewhere in the region of 3 – 5 g of almost pure cocaine a day, so I reasoned that if I was smoking crack, then I surely wasn't sticking as many pins in my body. To my mind, it had to be better than what I had been doing, but the truth was I had become completely hooked on both and over the course of 24 hours probably injected just as much as before.

In the end, I was spending hundreds of pounds a day to feed my various habits of crack, cocaine and alcohol, which wasn't a financial problem, as I had thousands of pounds at my disposal. What did prove a dilemma, in the midst of all this mayhem, was the £90k worth of drugs – which included a holdall full of cannabis resin – that needed to be taken care of. This, coupled with the constant threat of repercussion, mixed with increasing levels of paranoia driving me to near insanity, was where I think everything began to go seriously wrong.

* * *

Although Sykes and I had managed to find a safe enough stash for the drugs, it was only ever meant to be for a short period, and soon the hunt was on for somewhere more suitable. With all that was going on at the time, it was a hassle I could well do without, but a welcome answer to our problems soon arrived in the form of a man named Rolf. A trusted acquaintance of Fieder, Rolf and I had been introduced some weeks before and I quickly became very good friends with him – more friendly, I think, than with Fieder, and in some respects more than with Palsy, too.

Weighing up the situation I suddenly found myself in, and having a good feeling about it, I went to Rolf and more or less told him what had happened with the robbery. It was a gamble, for sure, as I had no idea how he would respond to such a confession, but at the same time I really felt I had no choice. Palsy was completely oblivious to what Sykes and I had done, and that was the way I wanted it to stay, and Sykes ... Well, he just couldn't be trusted.

As far as I was concerned, I had to let someone else in on it, not only for the purposes of a safe stash, but for something much more than that. You see, I was very aware of how vulnerable I had become and of the need for some form of protection, and this is where Rolf came into it.

Rolf was a hard man. He was well respected inside and outside of The Pond and extremely handy – as well as willing – when it came to the violent side of things, although this was something I wasn't completely adverse to myself. However, I felt somewhat powerless, not knowing the extent of what might be waiting for me, so it made perfect sense to bring him onside, if I could only cajole him into my affairs.

Now, I completely manipulated the whole situation to suit that particular need. I purposely dragged the poor guy into something he had absolutely nothing to do with by dangling a carrot in front of his face, something far too tempting for him to refuse. If he would stash our drugs – which as far as he was aware, from the information I had given him, had been acquired by default from an unknown source – and keep them somewhere safe along with his own, then he could help himself to whatever he wanted, whenever he wanted, and keep whatever profit he made. To most people in our line of work, this would have been a dream come true.

Personally speaking, it wasn't really that big a sacrifice for me, as I had little interest in the drugs at the time. As far as I was concerned they were a liability more than anything else, and a millstone round my neck, but to Rolf they presented an excellent opportunity to make a lot of money. He had access to all the drugs he wanted, and I had someone onside who, if it all went wrong, would be instantly implicated, meaning I would not be alone.

Yes, by doing someone he had begun to think of as a close friend a good turn, Rolf had inadvertently placed himself in a situation where my concerns were every bit as much his.

That winter of 1999 saw the whole crack craze explode; just about everyone I knew was at it. I was at it, Sykes was at it from time to time – although he much preferred the needle – and before long even Rolf was at it, although that was something I never intended to happen. But then, such was the extent of my personal usage that it was bound to spill out around me. It certainly ended up affecting more people than ever was my intention.

The weeks and months leading up to Christmas that year were complete and utter madness. I was overdosing regularly, sometimes two or three times a day; the crack pipe was never far from my mouth, or the syringe from my veins. The vodka and coke I drank all day long had become my main source of nourishment, and how my body managed to keep going I will never know; there were many times, it has to be said, that it very nearly didn't.

Overdosing had become a regular occurrence and was something I will admit to having done quite deliberately on more than one occasion. As I sit here now, typing out these words, I can only thank God for helping me through those situations, because I can't honestly think, for the life of me, how else I could possibly have survived them.

I recall one incident, which happened while visiting my friend, Martin, at his apartment in the city centre. The two of us were standing in his kitchen, directly in front of the cooker. It was early evening, and I had just administered hit number whatever, and almost immediately I knew I had OD'd. I threw out my hands and grabbed the top of the cooker firmly, in preparation for what would undoubtedly follow.

Realising what was about to happen, Martin stood behind me, holding tight onto my shoulders just as it began. I was then thrown backwards and forwards with the convulsions, my heart trying to rip itself from my chest for what seemed like ages, until eventually the fit began to subside, leaving me wrapped up in Martin's arms and legs, totally unable to move, with poor, old Martin completely sandwiched between the cooker and me, and the wall behind him.

Viewing the scene afterwards, we noticed that although he had been holding onto me, and he certainly wasn't a weakling, in the mere 30 to 40 seconds that the fit lasted, I had managed to shake the cooker, with Martin on my back, about a foot and a half from the wall. It stopped only because of the power cable, and very possibly the wall behind us. That was how sudden and how powerful an overdose could be.

* * *

There was certainly a lot going on with me at that time, both physically and mentally, as I daily experienced some truly awful effects of the drugs, but there was also something going on that I didn't quite know what to make of, and it was something of a spiritual nature.

Now, you might be wondering how on earth I can go from overdosing to the supernatural in one paragraph, but there is no question in my mind that the two are intrinsically linked. Drugs, I firmly believe, can open portals into other realms.

If the overdose itself wasn't bad enough, what quite often came with it – wherever it was from – most definitely was. Here is just one example ...

I was on my own at the flat of a friend who was working nightshift. Having borrowed his keys earlier that day, I had gone to his apartment late that night to use it as a chill out while he worked. Being a Welshman, he thankfully had a CD by the Manic Street Preachers, which I had playing in the background as I sat counting out all the money I had made. I then had a couple of hits and sat drinking the best part of a bottle of vodka, before deciding to have a lie down prior to heading into town and going through it all again in a matter of hours when The Pond reopened.

I emptied the contents of my pockets onto the floor next to the bed – mobile phones, cocaine, syringes, tobacco; the sum lot of my life really – as that morose feeling descended upon me like a dark cloud, which it always did at the end of the day.

It must have been somewhere in the region of 3 a.m. as I lay there in near darkness, the only light coming from a street lamp outside. Having prepared a hit, I took a few deep breaths and then sent it on in, with the intention of it being the last of the night. Almost immediately I knew I had taken too much. It completely missed out any build up and instead threw me straight into convulsions. Flying backwards onto the bed, I quickly grabbed hold of the mattress at either side of me. Within seconds I was gasping for breath, trying as hard as I could to take control of my breathing. If successful, this would quite often be enough to bring me out of the fit, but my body was in complete spasms. It was by far the worst seizure I had experienced so far, made doubly worse by the fact I was on my own.

It was then, in the middle of this terrifying attack, that I noticed someone – or something – standing on the landing, just outside the bedroom door. In amongst the darkness and these body-wrenching spasms, I was aware of a presence; something was watching me.

I pulled tighter on the mattress and strained my neck to see what it was, almost tearing my muscles in the process, and the more I managed to focus on it, the more it seemed to take on a form.

Now, this was by no means the first time I had been aware of a presence, or even that I'd seen something apparition-like, but on this occasion I could almost make out what it was. I could see its shape, where its head was, its arms and shoulders, and it was completely black – much blacker than the blackness of the hallway. I then noticed that it was wrapped in a cloak, and that its left arm was stuck inside it, as if concealing something. I also noticed that although it was looking towards me, it wouldn't look directly at me, preferring instead to hide its face, which I was glad about.

At this point I wanted to turn away, but I couldn't take my eyes off it; I suppose I was just too frightened. Also, after all this time, and the many hallucinations of this kind that I'd had, I was in a sense grateful to finally see what had always been just out of sight, lurking in the darkness at the corners of my eyes.

Lying there, holding on as tightly as I could, my body trying to rip itself up from the bed, I knew I couldn't let go.

I couldn't let it take me. In between the gasps for breath, I began shouting at it, trying to coax it into making a move, and every time I opened my mouth it would jerk a little towards me, like a spider tweaking at the threads of its web. I felt very small and helpless lying on that bed, while that phantom-like creature in the doorway watched me, waiting to pounce. But, as helpless as I knew I was, I somehow became aware that it was unable to do anything, because I was still alive.

I turned away from the door, still gasping and struggling to breathe, hoping that this would end, but when I looked back it was still there, exactly the same, only perhaps a little closer. I turned away a second time, my heart almost exploding within me, and cried out to God for help!

And just then, I was struck by yet another presence. Either inside of the curtains, which were a little above my head and to the right of me, or just outside of the curtains, I could see the silhouettes of three heads looking down at me – which was very strange, as I was in a second-floor apartment – and then, just as quickly as the convulsions came, everything began to slowly calm.

Lying absolutely still, my grip loosening on the sweat-soaked bed, I wondered what on earth they were. Then somehow I seemed to sense what they were thinking. Their thoughts penetrated my mind and I was aware that they were full of sorrow for me, full of pity. I lay there on the bed staring at them, unable to look away, until the silence became silence once more, and the darkness of the room became just that.

* * *

I seemed to exist in a twilight world, blending in with the shadows, virtually unseen in the daylight hours, flitting between bars and nightclubs, spending as little time in the open as possible. As a result, I grew to depend upon the cover of darkness; it was where I felt safe, hidden from the eyes of those who perhaps sought me. There was no question that other powers – powers I had no real understanding of – were at work.

No, it wasn't all about the abuse I was putting my body through, or even the paranoia; rather, there was an acceptance of those forces I knew were lurking in the near-death experiences encountered on the path I so readily chose.

By the end of November, the whole paranoia thing was completely out of hand. Sykes was running around with a Smith and Wesson 6 shot revolver stuffed inside his jacket, ready to shoot whoever. I was thinking and seeing things that were really very disturbing, although perfectly content as long as I had a lump of crack and a couple of 5-ml syringes in my pockets. But Rolf didn't seem to be handling things well, at all; in fact, he quickly became a major cause for concern.

Both Fieder and I had noticed a dramatic change in Rolf. He had quickly gone from being a cheery, fun guy to be around to a psychotic party pooper. He didn't trust anyone anymore; he was always very accusatory; he began making some rash business judgements and, to top it all off, he simply wouldn't listen to advice. He began doing more and more of his dealings in private and from his house, which wasn't like him. He was also increasingly in possession of larger and larger amounts of drugs, and he'd found himself a little helper, a man named Smiffy, who he had managed to talk into doing all his running around for him.

I could quite understand everything that was happening to him, the mistrust, the accusations, even having someone to do your business for you. After all, it made life a lot easier when someone else was doing the picking up and dropping off. But when that someone happened to be an oilrig manager? Yes, the crack epidemic was reaching a lot of different people groups, and it certainly wasn't choosy about who it took a hold of, but that didn't mean that everyone was cut out for it.

Although I didn't particularly care for this set up, I got on quite well with Smiffy, most of the time, but it became fairly obvious to both Fieder and I that he simply didn't have a clue what this was about! And when he began interfering in our business, trying to give advice in matters he wasn't qualified in, it grated on our nerves. Neither Fieder nor I liked how that particular partnership was working, and I think we both saw the danger signs well in advance, but Rolf just wouldn't listen.

I recall one instance when Rolf had sent Smiffy to pick me up from my girlfriend's flat to take me to the stash. It was a Saturday morning, and I needed some bits and pieces. I jumped into the car, put on the seatbelt and thanked him for doing me this particular favour at such short notice. He looked at me strangely, and then started to question me about my friendship with Rolf, making out that Rolf was really annoyed with me and that I needed to sort my head out, or something along those lines.

I simply couldn't believe what I was hearing from him, this sad, old man, who was nothing more than a glorified chauffeur and who was risking his neck, his career even, for a blast on a crack pipe!

Not in any mood for his rubbish, I brushed it aside, as I really couldn't be bothered to argue with him, but as I buckled up the seatbelt I felt one of my feet hit something on the floor. I looked down and to my utter horror saw two quarter-kilo bars of cannabis resin just lying there.

I turned on him angrily. "What do you think you're doing, picking me up with *that* in the car?"

He looked at me like I was going soft or something.

"What do you care, PJ?" he replied, rather smugly.

The reality of the situation was that we might easily have been pulled over by the Drug Squad, and I simply wasn't in the habit of putting myself at any unnecessary risk. What's more, I certainly wasn't in the mood to be talked down to by him!

To save further argument, I opened the glove compartment to put the bars away and couldn't believe what I saw next. It was absolutely crammed full of ecstasy tablets! These tablets came in vacuum-packed batches of two thousand, and clever clogs sitting next to me must have poured in the entire contents of a bag – hence the reason the cannabis had been thrown on the floor!

I yelled at him to stop the car and told him in no uncertain terms what I thought of him and how lucky he was that I didn't rip his mouth open. Following that, I ordered him to have the car cleaned up, then go home and have a little think to himself about whether he was in the right line of business or not. Then I slammed the door shut behind me, deciding it would be much safer to get a bus, or even walk.

Later that day I spoke to Rolf, who said something like: "Oh, yeah, Smiffy told me about your 'little tantrum' earlier today. He hopes you manage to get over it."

I was absolutely boiling at the mention of my "little tantrum". I fully understood that Smiffy was helping him out and taking a lot of the risk, too, but why this imbecile was being trusted with large amounts of drugs and money, when he clearly didn't have a clue what it was about, was beyond me.

"What you want to do, Rolf, is get rid of that clown!" I said, meaning it as a good bit of advice and nothing more.

Rolf simply laughed it off, patted me on the back, and made me out to be "over reacting".

Unfortunately for Rolf, a few weeks after the incident with Smiffy, the concerns that Fieder and I often aired between us were realised, as Rolf was finally busted. The Drug Squad had been watching us for quite some time, which we were well aware of, but on this particular morning, knowing there was a good chance he would have been drinking, they pulled him over at the side of the road at 2 a.m. As luck would have it, they discovered that he wasn't only well over the limit, but that the car was saturated with drugs.

The police then made a further search of his house, with him present, and turned up a lot more drugs, mostly small, snappy bags containing cocaine, some of which he had even forgotten was there. Ironically – although not surprisingly – the wonderful Smiffy was also arrested. He apparently walked straight into the middle of the search, waving a quarter-kilo bar of cannabis above his head, thinking there was some kind of party going on.

They were both charged, held in the cells and let out a day or two later. However, on release they had more or less gone straight to the stash, where they were swooped on a second time, which really was game over. They were eventually released on bail and only then were we able to find out the full extent of what had gone on.

Rolf had been charged with everything from faulty brake lights to the supply of drugs. To tell the truth, it had all happened so quickly, and with such devastating results, that I was in shock for days after.

Everything was gone, the entire stash of drugs. As they'd discovered such a vast quantity, and because Rolf had so much evidence stacked against him, along with previous convictions, his lawyer warned him that he was possibly looking at a double figure sentence.

My world simply crumbled with that news, not because we had lost all the drugs, but because of what had happened to Rolf. I'd been trying my best to make him see sense and get him to put his house back in order, and after all that had taken place I felt completely and utterly responsible.

* * *

It was Christmas Day and Rolf, who was awaiting trial and still managing to do a little graft with cocaine – he was being supplied from a source in Liverpool – had invited a few close friends to join him for dinner at an expensive hotel on the west side of town. I woke that morning at my girlfriend Helen's, not particularly in the mood for it, but not wanting to let him down. So I decided to make an effort. After all, it hadn't been easy for him to make the reservation and, of course, there was a very good chance that it might be some time before he enjoyed a Christmas with his friends again.

I left the flat at Woodside and walked down George Street, where a freezing, cold wind stung my face. Every now and then a car would pass by with all these happy-looking people inside: mum and dad in the front, the kids in the back, laughing and carrying on, knowing they would soon be in a nice, warm house enjoying each other's company, opening their presents. In truth, it made me more than a little sad.

When I arrived at the hotel a little late for dinner, after eventually managing to flag down a taxi, there they all were at the table: Fieder, Rolf, Gus, Shamus – a real motley crew, if ever I saw one. They all turned and watched me as I weaved through the sea of tables.

"You look like you had a good night!" Fieder commented, as I approached.

A silence followed and immediately I detected an atmosphere that I couldn't be bothered with. I took off my jacket, sat down and ordered some drink and whatever I fancied on the menu from the hovering waiter.

"What do you mean?" Rolf said in a drunken, slurring, contemptuous attempt at a welcome. "PJ always has a good night! *Don't you, PJ?*" he half shouted, leaning across the table towards me.

I didn't say a word. I simply looked away and glanced instead round the hall at all those happy people enjoying their day out. Then the tray of drinks arrived and I knocked back some vodka, a feeling of sadness rising up in me once more. I glanced quickly round the table, stood up and went to the toilet to have a hit. I had to do something about the melancholy that was eating away at me.

Thankfully, there was no one in the toilets and so I managed to take some clean water from the tap straight into the syringe, instead of using water out of the toilet bowl, for example. I then went into the cubicle where I locked the door and pushed my foot tight up against it.

Every now and then someone would come in or go out, and every time that happened I could hear children yelling, babies crying, and men and women laughing and shouting. To me, that afternoon, the noise outside the toilet was deafening and sitting in that cubicle was the best place in the world to be.

After administering the hit, I sat there for a few moments, huffing and puffing, until I was satisfied that I hadn't OD'd, then I left the toilets and walked back out into the hall, where I was met by total silence. It was as if everyone had completely stopped what they were doing.

The door shut behind me with a crashing bang, and then I heard a man's voice speaking somewhere to my left. Looking around, a little startled, I saw a magician doing tricks on the floor, with about 40 children sitting in a semi-circle around him. Glancing to my right, I saw a sea of tables surrounded by people with big, red, round faces, all watching the show. Suddenly it became deafening again.

I dropped my head and walked straight on, not wanting to meet anyone's eyes, until I had no choice but to look up. I could see my associates all watching me, shaking their heads in disapproval, apart from Fieder who thought it was priceless. I looked down at my feet and saw a drop of blood fall from my hand, but I kept walking towards them, as the cold liquid ran down the inside of my arm.

And it seemed like everyone in that room was laughing – everyone, except me.

* * *

The New Year came and a new Millennium began, but I didn't hold out much hope for it at all. As far as I could see, there was nothing to give me any reason to believe that this year would be any better than the last.

Rolf was facing a long stretch in prison; Smiffy had left the country and was hiding out somewhere in Russia with his Russian wife; Palsy was still extremely dependent on me, which wasn't a good thing, and certain people were hatching plans to exact revenge; I had a massive cocaine thing going on and I really didn't like any of it any more.

I just wanted it all to end. I was a complete shadow of a man and almost certainly on the verge of a serious breakdown, until a friend by the name of Catherine stepped in to try to help me.

Catherine was a rather successful business lady, who I'd met on a few occasions through my cocaine dealing. We had become quite good friends, with me visiting her at her house now and then, even calling along to her many social gatherings, where I would supply cocaine to her friends.

After a while I began to trust her, and she began to understand more about what it was I did for a living. At first she always saw me in a good frame of mind, but more and more towards the end of that year, and certainly into the beginning of the next, as she got to know me better she began to see the other side of what I did. She saw the tears, the pain, the threats and the violence connected with my lifestyle and, as a result, she eventually stopped having her plush little parties. She also stopped buying cocaine, probably to the annoyance of her friends, as her conscience simply wouldn't allow it any longer. Meeting me, and seeing the flip side of what went on in the world of drugs, changed her way of thinking.

In March 2000, I went to live with her, and within a matter of days it was decided that I really needed to get out of Aberdeen and away from everyone around me. And so, a plan was devised to send me off to Southern Spain, where I would live with a friend for the unforeseeable future, or at least until I had my head sorted out.

CHAPTER 7

I arrived back in Aberdeen in mid-July 2000, having lasted as little as three months in the beautiful coastal regions of Southern Spain. Sadly, things hadn't worked out the way that Catherine and I had hoped they would; in fact, they ended up every bit as much of a carry-on as anything that had gone before. For instance, I had been arrested by the Guardia Civil – not very a nice experience – on three separate occasions, and I was being hunted by a gang for my involvement in the robbery of a taverna in the extremely patriotic village of Frigiliana.

By the time Catherine eventually agreed to rescue me by bringing me back to Aberdeen, I was hiding out near a dusty, little town called Calahonda and living out of a ramshackle tent buried deep in the middle of some woods, having really upset some ex-pats in the village of Benalmadena Pueblo (something to do with a car chase through the village, in which a lot of damage was done to one or two parked cars).

In a relatively short space of time I had found myself in a precarious situation, where I was wanted in just about every town and village between Nerja and Fuengarola, and I was left with no other choice but to make my exit as fast as I could. The Costa del Sol very quickly became the "Costa Too Small". Too much sun – and far too much cheap vodka!

Once back in the relative safety of Aberdeen, Catherine's offer to me was very simple. I was to live with her in her great, big house and she would help me try to figure out a positive plan for my future. It was a condition of sorts. Having brought me back to Aberdeen at such short notice, and at quite an expense, too – especially considering how much rubbish I'd worked while out there – her subsequent treatment of me certainly didn't reflect the disappointment she'd felt, instead it went far beyond the call of duty.

I was given my own bedroom and bathroom, and had complete freedom of both the inside of the house and the garden. On top of all that, Catherine always made sure I had all the alcohol I needed. A bottle of Jack Daniels and a dozen bottles of Budweiser were constantly replenished when required, plus I could help myself to whatever food I wanted, whenever I wanted. It really was quite remarkable that I should have landed in such luxury, considering all that had gone on, but such was Catherine's concern for my wellbeing that it seemed nothing was too much for her.

Feeling somewhat guilty, I did try to help pay my way by promising to strip the paint from the wooden panelling of the Victorian bay windows, and where possible assist the painter and decorator with the refurbishments she was having done to her house. Not being in a position at the time to financially contribute, I felt it was the least I could do, although it was never once stipulated that I had to do anything.

Catherine appreciated the gesture and was greatly encouraged that I was keen to do something for her, but behind this overwhelming demonstration of generosity and trust, there was most definitely a catch. Ultimately, what Catherine sought from this setup was not that I should work my ass off around the house trying to earn my keep, or that she would continue to spoil me for the rest of my life; no, what she really hoped for was that over a period of time, with her guiding influence, I would begin to wean myself off this self-destructive mindset and want to live a more normal life. This took a little while to register with me, but by the time it did, I was so very grateful for her help, regardless of whatever motives lay behind it. It was, however, an extremely big ask – far bigger, I think, than either of us knew.

Things set off on a reasonably good footing. We got along fairly well, most of the time, and always had a good laugh together. However, there were times that Catherine became a little frustrated, when it must have seemed that I wasn't trying very hard or taking her seriously. For example, she would go out to work every morning, quite happy to leave me at home alone, but the minute she left I would rise from my bed, go downstairs and start drinking. By the time she arrived home from work in the evenings, after a hard day in the office trying to run a major company, I would merely have warmed up the electric paint stripper and without fail I – and on occasion the decorator, too – would be drunk.

Catherine didn't particularly appreciate arriving home to find me in a drunken state, and was at times a little vocal about it, but she fully understood that the changes she believed would come weren't going to happen overnight, and falling out with me over it wasn't going to help.

So, that was just how things were for at least two months. I never went hungry and certainly never wanted for a drink, living very comfortably, safe and secure, within the confines of Catherine's home. But the truth was that what was going on within me was something quite different. Yes, I was happy, most of the time, but I was desperately lonely and constantly drifting in and out of varying degrees of depression, which I tried hard to mask with the constant use of alcohol.

To be honest, I don't think we were ever fully convinced that her plan would work out, but neither of us ever said as much, even during our many in-depth conversations. I had a roof over my head, Catherine had her little project, and whatever would be would just have to be.

As time passed, more and more each day I would find myself at one of the windows working with the paint stripper, or just out of boredom watching people make their way to and from the city centre, a 15-minute walk away.

With increasing feelings of loneliness, and many other needs building up in me, temptation finally won out. After almost three months of near solitude, never once in all that time even stepping outside the grounds of the house, I plucked up enough courage to visit a bar. Finding it such a relief, I began sneaking off every afternoon I could for a quick drink in The Short Mile, a quiet, little bar only a two-minute walk along the road.

It was all that was needed to quell the longings I had; just a couple of hours in a bar, talking with whoever happened to be there, even chatting up some female company. It was, without a doubt, the environment I was happiest in, but unknown to me these little excursions were having a noticeable effect on my behaviour, which soon caught Catherine's attention.

Yes, Catherine figured out what I was up to and as she'd been wrestling for some time about whether supplying me with alcohol every day was a good idea or not, she decided that hiding in the house all day long probably wasn't doing me much good either. So it was agreed that the best thing for me to do was find myself a job. We discussed the logistics of it and spent many a night scouring the local papers for any suitable work, then after a run of unsuccessful applications, my luck changed and at the beginning of November I was employed as a part-time barman in the Great Western Hotel, which was only five minutes from where we lived.

As liberating as that was to begin with, it unfortunately proved fatal, not only for Catherine's hopes for me and what she would have liked to achieve, but for our friendship, too. No sooner was I behind that bar than I met in with one or two people who were into cocaine, and everything spiralled into absolute mayhem.

I began contacting people I shouldn't and organising the odd deal here and there. I was quickly shooting up cocaine once more, after not having touched any since going away to Spain almost six months before, and as if that wasn't bad enough, I was doing it during working hours. I was also holding early morning lock-ins after the bar closed at night, inviting various friends to stay behind, much to the annoyance of a rather stroppy night porter, who after a few hours would eventually pluck up enough courage to throw us all out.

What initially began with nothing more serious than a line or two of cocaine with my newfound acquaintances, in no time at all turned me back into "the machine". It was truly incredible how it all managed to go off the rails so effortlessly, as if the previous months had counted for absolutely nothing.

Amazingly, the job lasted a couple of months, until after Christmas, when a lock-in too many meant I had to leave. With all that followed, it wasn't long into the New Year that Catherine found herself with no alternative but to throw me out. I was fully back to my old ways of smoking crack and injecting cocaine, while treating her with utter contempt.

Chance after chance she kept giving me, but time and again they were thrown back in her face. I would leave the house in the afternoon for a quick pint across the road and not return for days at a time, and when I did eventually show up, I would be completely wrecked. Catherine would usually lecture me after I'd had a chance to sleep it off and clean myself up, always warning me that it had to stop. But no sooner would she have said those words – and almost grovelling, I would have agreed – than my social security benefits would arrive, or a chance to make a little money on a quick deal would transpire, and I would be sneaking off out again. Naturally, Catherine soon grew tired of all the lies and finally she could take no more.

The end came after I had been out for a few days, ignoring all her calls and text messages asking me to go home to talk with her. On this particular occasion, I wasn't in a good place mentally. I had made quite a bit of money over those few days, and had participated in some really heavy drug sessions.

I remember being crouched up in a toilet cubicle in a bar somewhere near the city centre, my phone lying next to me on the floor, bleeping as yet another message came through. I picked it up and clicked to open the message, which simply read:

Peter, we really need to talk! Catherine.

I will never forget how I just laid that phone down, picked up the syringe lying next to me and stuck it into my vein, considering as I did this just how little value I placed upon my life, especially after using water from the toilet bowl to inject with – and not for the first time either.

A few hours later, at around four o'clock in the morning, after not speaking to Catherine for almost three days, I finally plucked up the courage to go home and face her. But instead of the door being open, as it normally would have been, it was locked. It was obvious to me then that Catherine had finally had enough, but being the kind of person I was, I broke into her house anyway.

Catherine found me some hours later, as she was about to leave for work, lying there on her dining room floor in a blood-stained T-shirt and jeans – the result of a few days of injecting, and whatever else I had been up to – and in no uncertain terms showed me the door for the very last time.

* * *

By March 2001, having dossed around various addresses throughout the city, while trying to work the odd deal here and there, I eventually managed to wheedle my way back into The Pond, and what's more, resume business almost exactly where I had left it nearly a whole year before. Fieder, who was absolutely overjoyed to see me returning, even managed to get me back onto the books with Itchy and Scratchy. Although I had reservations about that, at least it meant I had a regular drug supply.

Making myself known once more in Aberdeen city centre also meant that Palsy could at last return from whatever self-imposed exile he had set himself. Yes, my old friend, Palsy, had disappeared at roughly the same time as I had, which was perfectly understandable, as it was usually at my expense that he managed to survive in this game. When I had vanished off the streets, poor, old Palsy had been left with very little choice but to do the same.

Having enquired of his whereabouts over many days, and knowing he had to be somewhere in Aberdeen, I discovered the impossible had taken place in my absence and he was actually working. A rumour had surfaced that he was choking chickens in a chicken-processing factory, something I found very hard to believe, no matter how often I heard it. But it was soon verified when roughly three weeks later, he came walking in through the doors of The Pond, openly confessing to his time in the poultry business, much to everyone's amusement.

And so, by April things were back to their chaotic ways, and were almost identical to how they had been before I left Aberdeen – including the many ups and downs of a previous romance. Helen, who had been an on-off girlfriend during 1999, and almost right up until I went off to Spain, had also been happy to see my return. We'd had a rather turbulent relationship in the past, and possibly weren't much good for one another, but we were quite suited nonetheless, and deep down were really very fond of each other.

Well aware of the stuff I involved myself in, Helen was someone who had seen me at my worst on many occasions. She was also conscious of what had gone on before – the robbery and the quantities and kinds of drugs I dealt in – and at the same time was quite accepting of all those dubious characters I knocked around with, like Itchy and Scratchy, Rolf, Fieder and Palsy, to name but a few. She readily accepted these things, because she also knew the other side of me – the kind, gentle, and at times very romantic me.

By the time I met in with Helen again, she was in the process of being evicted from her council tenancy and so, after a spell of staying with various friends, we eventually moved into a flat together in one of the many hard-to-let areas of Aberdeen. It may not have been the nicest place to live, but it was only a ten-minute walk from the university, where Helen was one year away from completing a degree. It was also just a ten-minute walk from the school where she'd managed to gain a placement for Tony, her son from a previous relationship. He was about four years old at the time and would begin primary school once the summer holidays were over.

Finding myself part of a family unit, it became fairly obvious that I would have to try to change my ways. I promised to stop injecting and even to lay off the crack a little, although I wasn't quite ready to give up the drug dealing, unless, of course, I had a job that paid a decent wage.

Helen, though, was very patient, allowing me to do things at my own pace, and although it wasn't easy, within a few weeks I managed to cut down the crack binges to once or twice a fortnight and stop injecting altogether. I suppose having that something – or someone – worth living for made all the difference, although I did have a condition attached. As long I could go down the bar every afternoon, have a few drinks and at least 1 g cocaine, I could pretty much live with everything else! It was, without a doubt, a compromise of sorts, but with it Helen knew that I was more likely to try to behave myself.

Not long after the summer holiday period, as Tony began primary school, I decided that I needed help in this department, and so I made an appointment to see a doctor about my physical and mental wellbeing. I reasoned that if I was going to be responsible for Helen and her son, especially as he was starting school, then I needed to take life more seriously and try to set a better example for him.

Primarily the appointment was to have a liver function test and blood count, as recommended by my councillor at Drugs Action, where I had enrolled on a drug programme some time before. The idea was that if my body wasn't in too bad a condition, or was at least salvageable, then hopefully that would give me the incentive I required to really make a change, not only for Helen and her son's sake, but for my future health, too.

I have to admit that the changes I hoped to introduce weren't only to bring Tony up in a more stable environment, but were also to put to rest the feeling that had been bothering me for some time – that something serious was wrong with me. Every now and then I was aware of my liver throbbing, and although it was by no means painful, I would feel it pulsing away, sometimes for a couple of hours at a time, indicating that something wasn't quite right.

I think it was around that time that I first acknowledged there was a real possibility of me being hep C positive. Yet, whenever that thought entered my mind, as it sometimes did, I would fight against it, quickly dismissing it as a silly notion. I was somehow able to make myself believe that if I turned my life around, then everything would eventually be all right. As far as I was concerned, everything that was wrong with me would more than likely be put right by simply cutting down on my alcohol intake, and being more careful how I used drugs in the future.

But, of course, that depended largely upon receiving good news from the doctor. If the results went in my favour, as I dearly hoped they would, my plan was to eventually give up everything completely: drink, drugs, in fact, every vice imaginable. What's more, I would never go back to them again. It was actually something I got quite excited about, as I managed to convince myself that I would do it, although not everyone shared my enthusiasm.

I remember that morning, before going to see the doctor for the results, Helen and I walked Tony to school. On the way home, full of nervous excitement, I admitted to her what I had done, that I had been to the doctor, had given a blood sample, and would receive the results later that afternoon. As far as I was concerned, this was going to be a major turning point in my life. I really genuinely believed that.

"If everything turns out to be okay, Helen," I said, "I'll be giving up the drink and drugs forever!"

Helen stopped in her tracks, looked at my totally serious expression and laughed out loud, as she quite often would during discussions of this nature.

"Okay, Peter, but what if it's bad news? What then?" she replied, adding a touch sarcastically, "Will you just keep going until you're dead or something?"

That certainly wasn't what I wanted to hear that morning, and almost instantly I regretted telling her, although she was probably right. But I wasn't quite willing to consider that, having pinned my hopes on a good result. Things were going to change, regardless of Helen's scepticism, of that I was adamant.

But, of course, it didn't quite go as I would have liked.

* * *

"Now, Mr Jamieson, we're here for those results, aren't we?" Dr Hawking rifled through some papers. "You just wanted me to check your general wellbeing. No HIV or hep C test?"

"Yes, that's right."

"Okay. Your blood count is fine, your kidneys are fine, but I'm afraid your liver count is very high. Do you think you might have hepatitis?" he asked, knowing fine well that I didn't know the answer to that question.

"No, I don't think so!" I snapped back.

A silence followed, until I explained about having been checked after coming off heroin a few years before; the test results then had been negative.

He nodded, smiled a little, then went on to explain how serious it was to have a liver count as high as mine, firmly asserting that I would have to stop drinking and using drugs if I wanted to stand any chance of making a recovery.

Having asked a few questions about my alcohol intake, Dr Hawking then quickly calculated the amount of alcohol I consumed in a normal week. This turned out to be between four and seven bottles of vodka and about 60 to 90 pints of lager. He was horrified to learn that most weekends I would start on a Friday morning and – fuelled with cocaine and crack – carry on sometimes without food and with very little sleep until Sunday or Monday. He simply couldn't wrap his head around the fact that people actually did those things.

Looking dismayed at my answers to his questions, he was relieved to hear that I had stopped injecting, but when I told him how much cocaine I was still using, he just looked at me and scratched his chin. It worked out that I might use anything between seven and 21 grams a week – certainly never less than a gram per day. And then there were the crack binges, which could happen at any time and weren't necessarily restricted to the weekends. When the notion took me to smoke crack cocaine, which wasn't every night, I could end up smoking anything from 1 g to ¼ oz, and on a few occasions even more.

"How long do you think you injected cocaine before you finally stopped?" he asked.

"About a year, two years, maybe, on and off."

He sat back in his chair.

"Look, Peter, you really have got to make some changes to your lifestyle, there is nothing else for it, and what's more, you had better start now!"

He clasped his hands together in front of him and sat there looking at me, as if I was some kind of freak.

"Okay ..." I blurted out, feeling somewhat stupid in light of all that had been said "... what do you, as a professional in these matters, propose that I do about it, then?"

He leaned forward and took off his glasses.

"Peter, the best thing you can do when you leave here today is stop drinking, stop using drugs and, if you manage that, come back to see me in a few months and we'll check to see if there's been an improvement to your liver count."

There was yet another moment of silence between us.

"That's the best advice I can give you, Peter. Whether or not you follow it is entirely up to you, but if you carry on like this you could end up with cirrhosis of the liver, which can lead to cancer – but that's only if you don't somehow manage to kill yourself first!"

I left his office that afternoon incensed, and went straight to Specky's Bar where I drank large vodkas until it was time to meet with Itchy's "runner" – a person who carries drugs – to pick up my next batch.

Needless to say, nothing much changed and I carried on as before, which didn't come as any surprise to Helen, of course. I grafted for Itchy and co., drank vodka, snorted cocaine, had the odd crack binge, and was forever in and out of varying degrees of debt. But every waking day thereafter was a challenge; it was a case of damage limitation.

* * *

In September 2003, Helen and I were married in the university chapel and life, at last, began to show signs of having a bit of normality about it. After all, I wasn't only a husband (once more), but had become a father figure to a wonderful six-year-old boy, who deep down I wanted to influence in a positive manner!

Taking it all seriously, as one should, the first thing I tried to do was spend less time in the bar and more time at home. It was a gesture greatly appreciated by Helen and something that made me feel a little better about myself, although it did have its problems.

Trying to do the decent thing meant that it took me longer to sell my drugs, which placed me under constantly increasing pressure from Itchy, but I was certainly drinking considerably less and getting away with using little more than 1 g cocaine a day. Not giving in to Itchy's demands was difficult, but I ploughed on ahead regardless, trying hard to focus on a more positive plan for our future.

I then surprised everyone by enrolling on a three-day Banksman Slinger course, which just as surprisingly I managed to complete successfully. In the weeks that followed, I found myself working for an employment agency, ripping out the inside of the old House of Fraser building on the corner of Market Street. I was still dealing drugs, in case things didn't work out, but I wasn't sitting in The Pond morning, noon and night. I now had a life away from there, which had the potential to completely change things.

After a couple of months of demolition work – something I really enjoyed – I was compensated for my efforts by being awarded a full-time position working in the pipe yard of a major oil company. It was, without a doubt, one of the best things ever to happen to me. I was working with a fantastic bunch of guys; the canteen was free; the food was excellent, and the wages were very reasonable. In fact, I honestly couldn't have asked for better.

Sadly, it all came crashing down after only three months, when I not only lost my position at the oil firm, but was kicked out of the agency after failing a random drug test.

Losing that job when I did, and in the manner I did, had a totally negative effect on me. After all, I had put myself through some rigorous tests and had worked myself into favour with an agency by proving to be reliable, willing and hardworking. I'd then been rewarded with a permanent contract at Total, one of the biggest oil companies working in the North Sea, with all the perks that went along with it, only for it to be cruelly taken away by my dependency on drugs. What that did to me, more than anything, was prove that no matter how hard I might try in life, I would always fail. My heart sank, my head went down, and I immersed myself once more in the drug trade – much to Itchy's relief.

* * *

As a family, regardless of what I did for a living, we just learned to get on with it. Tony lived a perfectly normal life, was even spoiled a little in many ways, and Helen undertook all the duties of a caring mother and wife. She took Tony to school in the mornings and picked him up again in the afternoons, she cooked and she tidied and generally kept the house running, although in amongst it all she also found plenty of opportunity to join me in whatever I might be doing, whether it was drinking ... or whatever.

I suppose there were times when Helen absolutely hated what I did, but there were also times when she enjoyed it, too. I was just never really sure what frame of mind she was going to be in from one day to the next, accepting or not. What might be deemed okay one day wasn't always okay the next; something might be fine for a whole week and the next it wasn't. To be honest, I was just never very sure what to expect from her, and so it became easier for me to do the wrong thing all the time, so that when it was deemed acceptable by her, it would be a good time for us both.

Yes, life was rather chaotic, as I tried to juggle what I did for a living on a run-down, drug-ridden council estate, while at the same time trying to keep a sense of normality about it, for Tony's sake, at least. I suppose we just learned to live with our lot, as awkward as it sometimes was, with the hope that it didn't affect Tony's upbringing.

By the beginning of 2005, the writing was very clearly on the wall for us as a married couple. It had been a tough time emotionally, with me leaving home on a couple of occasions, due to us not getting along very well. We were also in a mess financially, because of various debts I had run up to a couple of gangs. But the icing really landed on the cake when the Serious Crime Squad decided it was about time to pay me a visit.

It was a Saturday evening, and some neighbours had allegedly reported seeing a gang of Scousers at my door with guns, which was possible, considering how much money I owed people. But this act of neighbourly kindness resulted in nothing more than our flat being raided. Helen and I were arrested, stripped searched and released a few hours later on nothing more serious than a possession of cocaine charge. Considering what normally went on in our flat, it wasn't anywhere near as bad as it might have been, had they gone about things a little differently, but it certainly didn't help our relationship.

To make matters fully worse, two days after the raid we had a visit from the CID (Criminal Investigation Department) who suspected I was withholding vital information concerning a murder that had taken place over that same weekend. I'd had absolutely nothing to do with the murder in question, and I think they knew that, too, but they weren't so sure about my Scouse visitors, and when I thought a little more about it, neither was I. It certainly put me in a rather difficult position.

I wasn't an evil person, at least, I never condoned the use of violence, but having worked for these gangsters for so many years, I could hardly say I was completely innocent of all matters concerning it. There were plenty of people who ended up hurt and some of them quite seriously, although I always tried my hardest to distance myself from that. But, suddenly finding myself with two officers sitting across from me in my own home, believing that I was somehow involved in it, really affected me. I wasn't particularly worried, as I was completely blameless on this occasion; I was more upset that they thought I might be capable of such a thing in the first place. It caused me countless problems in the weeks that followed, and not only with my conscience, but also for my business, as I knew I was being watched.

So, over the space of one weekend, life became more difficult than ever. A series of unfortunate events simply dragged me down lower than I could have imagined possible, and nothing seemed to go right after that. The crack binges increased by levels of magnitude; having crack users living in almost every flat surrounding us – upstairs, downstairs and directly next door – meant there was just no getting away from it. My alcohol and cocaine consumption went through the roof, too, and as a result our marriage teetered on the brink of collapse.

However, what affected me most at that time were the deaths of a few friends through suicide. These seemed to happen almost one after another, over the space of little more than 12 months. It was such a depressing time.

Yet, as hard as that was to take, I could totally understand it. Every morning for well over a year I'd been waking up and contemplating doing the exact same thing; in fact, it was the very first thought to enter my mind each day. As soon as I opened my eyes, I would feel my heart sink as a profound heaviness grabbed hold of it and dragged it down, and then the desire to take my life was very real, indeed.

I would lie there in bed, or wherever I happened to wake up, listening to my heartbeat. I would try not to breathe for long periods of time, concentrating on my heart as hard as I could, willing it, inwardly pleading with it, to just stop. Knowing this would never happen, I would then picture myself rising and tying up a rope to the light fitting in the ceiling, pulling a noose down around my neck, and kicking the chair away.

It actually got to the stage where I had to visualise myself dying in this manner before I could face the day. Don't ask me why that should have been, but going through that same ritual each morning somehow gave me the strength I needed to carry on, even if it was for just one more day.

* * *

As unhappy as I may have been about the various predicaments I found myself in, I really have to give credit to Helen for trying her hardest to hold everything together. For quite some time, she had watched me plummet downwards, and had done all that she could to help.

I don't think Tony even knew me anymore. I was forever out and about doing my own thing and even when I was at home, which was seldom, I would be completely wrecked, on the drink and using crack whenever possible. It was obvious to a lot of people that I needed help, but what could they do?

But then, around this time, some events unfolded that took me by surprise and offered me my greatest means of escape. I awoke one day to news from my sister in Shetland saying I was going to inherit quite a lot of money! Plans were afoot that would see me receive a fair share of our inheritance, and it couldn't have come at a better time for me.

Being seriously in debt was a major hurdle, so the news about the money – the grand sum of £26,000 – was the lifeline that was required! It was certainly a cause for celebration, and we did plenty of that. I will never forget how happy Helen and Tony were when I told them that news; their beaming smiles simply said it all.

Yet, deep down inside, as wonderful as that news was, there was a fear in me that I had never experienced before. All I can say now is that the money – money I prayed would change my life – utterly destroyed me. It brought me to the lowest point in my life. Within six months of receiving that inheritance, I had destroyed my marriage, was sharing a flat with Rolf – who had been released from prison after serving almost five years of his sentence – and was back on the needle, drinking non-stop and smoking hundreds of pounds worth of crack a day.

A lot of good that did me, then! And yet, that's not exactly true, because I believe that if it hadn't been for that inheritance, I wouldn't be here to write this now.

When we first received the money I was in serious debt, not only to Itchy, but also to a gang from Glasgow, as well as a gang from Aberdeen. As always, I had my fingers stuck in so many pies, and through my constant use of cocaine and crack my debts had become completely unworkable. It was only a matter of time before someone decided to give me a proper doing.

Along with all that, my use of alcohol was at its peak, and my mental and physical wellbeing had deteriorated to such an extent that my drug councillor wanted to admit me for a stint in Cornhill Hospital, one of North East Scotland's primary mental health hospitals. I had actually volunteered for this service – basically a ten-day detox with counselling – some time before, while I was with Helen. I had been on the waiting list for some time, but by the time they called me to go in, it was too late. I had received my inheritance, was indulging in all manner of drug sessions, and I simply refused.

As soon as that money had gone into our account, I had started paying off my debts. I remember telling Helen that although I would pay what I owed, I didn't want my father's inheritance to be wasted on drug debts, and so would use some of the money to make the loss back again. So, rather than simply paying off the four or five thousand pounds I owed to various people, I "reinvested" in drugs, thinking I would make back whatever money I'd had to fork out. Once I'd done that, I'd give it up forever.

Try as she might, Helen just wasn't able to make me see sense, that I should just make a clean break from the drug dealing altogether and accept the losses, such as they were. All she could do, in total frustration, was stay well out of the way and hope I would at least do what I said I would: only continue until I had replaced the money I had paid out on debts. But it didn't stop there; the dealing – and the using – just went on and on and on.

Throughout that time, it was always in the back of my mind just how much the money should have meant to me. After all, my father had worked hard, in fact, had *struggled* all his life to build something for his family. I fully appreciated that, but it seemed that the more I thought about what I was doing with it, the more it depressed me, and the more depressed I became, the more I tried to block out what I was doing. It didn't take long before it was no longer a life-changing sum of money. Within a month we were down to less than £20,000, and things just went from bad to worse.

By January 2006, Helen could stand it no more. Our marriage could no longer handle what was going on and the day came when it was finally over as, it seemed, was my life.

It was hardly surprising. Four months had passed and there was very little of the money left. Money aside, there was very little of me left either. I was hardly recognisable to Helen anymore. It was like living in a nightmare in which the person she loved was being consumed by something more powerful than either of us knew how to deal with.

We managed to see Christmas through together, more for Tony's sake than anything else, but we both knew that it was over for us. Helen just couldn't go on investing so much love in someone who wished his life away the way that I did; it was hurting her far too much.

For five years or more, Helen had lived this lifestyle. Through the many highs and lows, she had tried all that she could to hold it together, risking, it must be said, the welfare of herself and her only child. And why? Because she had genuinely loved me and hoped that there could be a future for us!

But eventually she had to let go.

* * *

It was a Friday night in April 2006, and I was alone at the flat. Rolf had begun working offshore again and was away on another two-week stint. I was sitting there, all by myself, a syringe in my hand and an empty bottle of vodka on the table. The "Manics" were singing on the stereo, and as usual they were singing about me, about my life.

The chorus rang out across the room: *"We don't talk about love; we only want to* get drunk *...!"*

There were tears in my eyes, my heart and my soul. I was as broken as I had ever known.

When I started this carry on, all those years before, probably before I even realised it myself, I had only ever been on a mission of self-destruction. There had been no room for sentiment in my life, nor any futile kind of emotion, and I had always been more than prepared to face the consequences of that. But, for some strange reason, no matter what I might throw at myself, I somehow kept hanging on.

I sat there thinking about my life, and I knew what it was that I had to do. Palsy, Fieder and Rolf ... They all came to mind.

Who do I have that really cares about me? I thought.

Earlier that day I had been out trying to collect some of the money that was owed to me, and it just made me so sad for everyone. Once again, within six months of receiving that money, I was in debt to Itchy and Scratchy for something like £7,000. Not only had I managed to blow my entire inheritance, I had accumulated another massive debt, one that I had no way of paying. And it had been plainly obvious to me that day - as I received one rubbish excuse after another - that no one was in any hurry to help me out.

I couldn't have cared less about the money, to be honest, as all I was ever really concerned about was being able to carry on using drugs and drinking, but what did seem to bother me was remembering how many times I had bailed each one of them out of trouble. Now, all of a sudden, one by one they were turning their backs on me. In the past I had received beatings and had put myself in some really tricky situations to try to help them, but for what?

I was fed up of it all. I was sick of their lies, sick of their self-importance, sick of their cowardice when they found themselves in trouble, and sick of their inept ability to deal with it, always having to look for someone to bail them out. All day long I had been in the company of these so-called friends, and I finally realised just how pathetic and empty it all really was.

It was over; I just couldn't go on anymore. I had lost everything; I had lost Helen and Tony; I had lost whatever respect I might have had for myself, as well as those around me. I just didn't feel that there was any reason to keep on living. I was 38 years of age, an alcoholic and a drug addict. I had no hope for the future, and not a friend left in this world, it seemed. And the one positive thing ever to have happened in my life – my father's inheritance – was squandered in a matter of months on drugs, alcohol and crap friends. As far as I was concerned, there was no point in carrying on.

I sat there on the edge of the sofa, listening to the words of a song as I prepared my last hit. It was quite dark in the room, the only light coming from the street lamps outside. I drew the solution up into the syringe and with a few deep breaths pushed it into my vein. And that's about as much as I can remember.

* * *

And so it was that a few hours later, on a Saturday morning in April 2006, I found myself in the back of an ambulance being rushed to Aberdeen Royal Infirmary. I remember looking up at the medic as he fumbled with various pieces of equipment, attaching them to my arm and chest, and wondering how it ever got to this.

Of course, I knew what I'd done to be in the back of the ambulance. I had injected myself with what I had hoped would be a lethal amount of cocaine, but it hadn't killed me like I'd perhaps hoped it would. I had undoubtedly gone into convulsions and fallen onto the floor, only to wake some hours later. I then managed to walk five minutes to a city centre bar, where they had eventually called the ambulance. That was roughly what happened – but why?

There were many reasons, but as I lay there in the back of the ambulance, I couldn't think of one. I simply couldn't remember what had prompted the attempted suicide. I suppose it must have seemed the right thing to do at the time. After all, I had yet another failed marriage to my name; I was an alcoholic, cocaine addict and crack addict; I was constantly haunted by my conscience for the things that I had done and for the kind of person I had become, and I felt completely broken inside. Perhaps those were my reasons.

As the ambulance dodged and weaved its way through the busy Saturday morning traffic, I lay there thinking about my life, as tears filled my dark and sunken eye sockets.

* * *

A few days later, I was back at Rolf's, sitting on the edge of my bed, looking at myself in the mirror, and what I saw frightened me. All I could see was emptiness – a void where a life had once been. I was also aware that I would have to somehow try to live with what I'd attempted to do, and the embarrassment of everyone finding out about it.

I sat there for what seemed like ages, contemplating suicide once more, but I couldn't, I simply *couldn't* have Rolf come home to find me hanging or something, it just wouldn't be fair on him. But I so dearly wanted to put an end to it.

Looking into those eyes shrouded with an overwhelming sorrow, I somehow remembered this young Christian man who often popped into The Pond after attending a Sunday evening service at Elim Church on Marischal Street. He always tried to speak to me about Jesus, and just then I remembered something he'd once said: "I go there every week to worship Jesus, because of all that He has done for us."

I didn't know if Jesus was real or not, or even if this stranger, who visited the bar on occasion, was being serious, but I lifted my head towards the ceiling and in my heart, as much as anything, I called out:

God, if you really exist, if you really are out there, then please, please, *will you help me now?*

I bowed my head and looked down at the carpet, having grown sick of my reflection in the mirror, and just then a thought came to my mind.

Peter, why don't you go home and see your sister?

My sister! But surely she wouldn't want anything to do with me.

Well, if there's nothing left for you but to take your own life, then why don't you at least go home and say goodbye? She was always there for you in the past. It's the least you could do.

And just at that moment, something inside my heart suddenly changed. I grabbed my wallet and found that I had enough money for the ferry home. I picked up my mobile phone and with a glimmer of excitement rising up within me, I called Palsy.

"Palsy ...? I'm really sorry, mate, but I have to go now."

CHAPTER 8

Arriving back in Lerwick at 7.30 a.m., on a cold and wet Friday in April, all of a sudden it didn't seem like the great idea it had been 16 hours or so before. There I was, standing outside the front of the ferry terminal, my bag slung over my shoulder, feeling a little like someone who had just returned from the trenches of the First World War. I felt rough and probably looked even rougher.

I also felt totally and utterly alone, a feeling that wasn't helped by the fact that from where I was standing I could see the rooftops of the street where I had grown up. It was such a sad sight to see, and hard to accept that I would never be back in that old house again, but the reality was there was no one there for me anymore. My father had been dead for almost seven years and my mother was in a care home, suffering from Alzheimer's. There was no longer such a thing as the family home, and no one to welcome me back.

My prospects for the rest of that day would have been bleak, had it not been for an invitation from a dear, old friend I'd grown up with all those years before on North Lochside. Neil had been travelling on the same overnight ferry and so we had joined company and spent the night together, drinking at the bar, discussing our respective situations, which were remarkably similar in many ways.

Neil's life had ended up much the same as mine; in fact, his was probably worse in some respects. He'd been kicked out of school at 14 and had then involved himself in alcohol and drugs, leaving Shetland and moving to London at roughly the same time as I left for Aberdeen – for almost identical reasons. Like me, he had spent the next 16 years of his life in various stages of addiction, interspersed with periods spent in prison, until finally moving back to Shetland some months before.

It had been a welcome surprise, meeting in with him prior to that particular journey, and the invitation to go with him that morning to his mother's house was one I was grateful for. We spent a pleasant day up in her attic lounge talking about the old days, about growing up as kids on North Lochside, about the docks and the things we used to get up to. We laughed about the endless trouble we always seemed to land ourselves in and needless to say we talked about that time he was rushed into hospital at five years old, after consuming all that alcohol behind the Garthspool Church.

Yes, thankfully Neil had survived his early encounter with alcohol, a couple of days in hospital the price he had to pay. However, it certainly hadn't endeared me to the other parents in our neighbourhood; being the elder of the two I had been blamed by just about everyone for what happened that day – though that was nothing unusual.

Now I was shocked to learn how dangerously close to death he had been. Apparently his mother was told that if he had lain for five minutes longer exposed to the cold, or if they hadn't received him at the hospital when they did, he would certainly have died. I suppose it was for this reason that his mother hadn't been quite so pleased to see me that morning, although she did ask me to make myself at home. This was a gesture I appreciated, and I showed my gratitude by drinking her house completely dry of any alcohol she happened to have in her cupboards.

How utterly ironic; there I was, my life in a complete mess through the scourge of addiction, getting drunk with the very first person I ever got drunk with all those years before, and infringing upon a lovely lady whose only son I had nearly killed. Which all caused me to wonder ... If only that had been enough to put us off for life, how different might things have been for us – a thought Neil's mother must have had a thousand times over the years.

* * *

By eight that evening, I had long since left the comfort of Neil's mother's home (much to her relief) and was drinking in Captain Flint's, probably the coolest bar in Lerwick town centre.

Standing alone with a drink in my hand, I gazed out of the window at the harbour below. It was raining hard and the town looked almost deserted. A few fishing boats were preparing to head back out to sea, the Bressay Ferry was coming in to dock, and directly opposite a few taxis waited patiently in the rank to pick up whoever was desperate enough to venture out on such a night.

I seemed to stand there for ages, oblivious to what was going on behind me, looking out over this familiar scene and continually going over some of the things that Neil and I had talked about. I couldn't help but feel sad.

Life in Shetland wasn't that bad, PJ. You had a good job and a wonderful girlfriend, but then you went and threw it all away, let it all slip through your fingers ...

I then dipped into a train of thought where it all began to make perfect sense.

Yeah, I know what I've lost. I know it only too well. And it really hurts now. But, hey, that's all right. It had to hurt sometime, PJ! It's just taken you the best part of fourteen years, that's all!

There was just so much that I could regret, but what was the point? It was all over.

What if you'd never moved away? What if you hadn't worked so much crap and not got so involved in the drugs? How might things have worked out for you then?

My thoughts could have tortured me, but I was no longer in a place where any of it really mattered anymore. It was all over and circumstances – people, even places – had long since moved on. Nothing was the same.

But as I struggled to convince myself that it really was all over, that I could never have any of that back, my thoughts swung back to my present situation, bringing me down to earth with an almighty thud.

What will everyone be thinking? Oh, how the mighty fall, PJ! Once the big man, but now look at you! And what will Itchy and Scratchy do when they find out you've disappeared owing them all that money? Think about it, PJ. What if this doesn't work out and you have no choice but to return to Aberdeen? What then?

Yes, the grip that Aberdeen had on me wouldn't even allow me to indulge in the self-pity I'd been blissfully soaking up; eventually it always dragged me back to its cold, granite streets.

There's going to be some very serious implications if this doesn't work out, PJ. You do understand that, don't you? It'll be a black bag at the bottom of the Mersey for you, boy. Maybe you should just get back to Aberdeen before anyone misses you and try to work things out. Forget this Shetland carry on, it's nothing but a waste of time. It'll only make matters worse. Perhaps Itchy will be a bit more understanding this time round.

And then, just as I was about to resign myself to the fact that this was all a waste of time, a rather gentler voice from out of nowhere tore me back to reality.

"Hiya, Uncle Peter!"

More than a little startled, I turned to see who it was.

"What are you doing here? Does my mum know you're here?"

At 18 years old, my sister's youngest daughter, Emma, was now drinking in the local pubs, and here she was standing before me.

"Eh, no, she doesn't!" I stuttered.

All of a sudden reality struck, instantly reminding me of the hopelessness of my situation and the reason I was there. To be honest, I didn't know what to think. Was I really ready to face my sister? Could I really change? Would she even want to help me?

I stood there, dazed and confused, looking at this rather excited young lady, not quite sure what I should say or do, until a small voice inside of me cried out: *Go and see your sister, Peter. She'll know what to do.*

Yes, I knew what it was I had to do, and wandering around drunk in a bar wasn't it.

* * *

My sister, Vera, had been busy all day – all week, in fact – working at one of the many music venues for the Shetland Folk Festival. At 8.30 p.m. she had merely popped home to put her feet up for an hour or two before going back to work.

"Hey, Mam!" Emma announced, as we walked in through her living room door. "Look who's here to see you!"

There was a look of complete surprise on my sister's face as we walked into the middle of the room. I smiled at her and sat down on the sofa.

Vera could tell that all wasn't well with me, so after exchanging a few pleasantries she asked Emma to go back out and leave us alone. She then made us some coffee and began telling me about the festival, about all the hours she had worked over the course of the week, the early starts, the late nights, and the countless meals she'd served.

"It seems like all I've said these last few days is 'would you like tatties or chips, tatties or chips, tatties or chips?'" she said, laughing a little.

I couldn't help but feel inwardly warmed by her good fun attitude. It was just like the Vera I had always known, her humour seemingly unchanged in the years that had passed, even by this sudden interruption to her evening.

Eventually she stopped speaking about her work and sat there looking at me.

"So what's happening with you, then?" she asked. "What's happened to Helen and Tony?"

At the mention of those names, I just couldn't help myself and I broke down before her.

"Peter, what's going on?" she said, sounding concerned.

I looked at her sitting across from me and took a deep breath.

"Helen and Tony ... Well, that's all over. I mean, they're fine and everything, and I'm all right about it. It's just everything else, Vera. It's me, it's my life ... I just can't go on like this anymore!"

Composing myself as best I could, I tried to explain to her about the last 20 years of my life, how it had been a complete lie and nothing more than a series of sad events. I told her about my problems as a youth; some she'd been well aware of and some, of course, she hadn't. I told her about the drinking and the drugs, how I'd had to leave Shetland, and how things had been like a helter-skelter ride after that. I told her about the heroin, showing her the remnants of scars and lumps on my arms and wrists.

I told her about the alcoholism, the depression, about the various trips to see doctors and drug councillors, and how nothing ever seemed to work. I told her about the cocaine and the crack, how it had very quickly, in my mind at least, turned me into a heartless monster, and then, ultimately, I told her how I had tried to commit suicide.

Vera listened intently, not saying a word until eventually I ran out of steam and things to say. She sat there quite silent, studying my face like never before.

"So, what about your dad's money, Peter?" she asked.

I looked down at my feet.

"How much of it have you got left?"

I looked up and watched her eyes as she waited for an answer, then shaking my head, I whispered, "None".

I saw the disappointment appear on her face the moment I answered, but strangely, she didn't look surprised. Then, after a moment's silence, she told me a story of her own.

"Oh, Peter, I never wanted to give you that money," she began. "Not like that, anyway. I knew it would be trouble. What I wanted to do was to hang on to it and give it to you in dribs and drabs, or at least keep it until I thought you were ready, but I was strongly advised against that. I was told that the best thing for us to do was just give it to you. At the end of the day, Peter, we'd no right to keep hold of your money. You were entitled to it, just the same as your brother and me. I suppose, if I'm honest, neither of us wanted you on our backs every time you wanted more. I'm so sorry!"

Vera sat there looking at me with tears in her eyes, wondering how that little boy she had helped to raise could end up making such a mess of his life. It was plain that she was greatly affected by it all.

"Look, Vera, it's all right, truly. What's happened has happened. There's no one to blame for all this but me. And the money ... Well, that can't be helped now."

Vera wiped her eyes and began to gather her emotions.

"Okay, so what now, Peter? What's next?"

What was next? I didn't know, and now that she'd posed the question ...

"Vera, I really don't know, but I was hoping that you might be able to help me."

She sat there in silence for what seemed like ages.

"In what way? I mean, how do you want me to help you?" she asked, an air of suspicion creeping into her voice.

"I don't really know, but one thing's for sure, I can't go on like this! Look, whether it's my body that gives in or I consciously do it myself, if I don't get out of this mess soon I *will* die. It just can't – *won't* – carry on like this!"

Vera could sense the inner workings of my mind and knew this was a crucial time for me.

"Okay, I'll think about it, Peter, but right now I'm going back to Islesburgh to help at the festival and I won't be back until the early hours of the morning. We'll speak again tomorrow."

* * *

The following day I woke quite early on the sofa I'd been allowed to spend the night on. I had been sweating and suffering with bad dreams, as usual, and I lay there feeling completely wiped out. In the unfamiliar surroundings of my sister's living room, my mind began racing back and forth, chewing incessantly over all the different scenarios that could be arising because I was in Shetland and not in Aberdeen, where some people would think I should be.

As I lay there, that familiar feeling of horror twisting and turning inside my stomach, my mind racing, while at the same time trying to shut itself down, thoughts of suicide began to fill my head ...

Standing alone on the deck, hands clasped around the railings, gazing out at the sun setting on the horizon, the freezing cold water of a wintry North Sea stretching out into the distance where the heavens meet the waves ...

As usual, I eventually mustered enough inner strength to give myself the mental slap that always brought me out of it, causing me to face the turmoil of yet another day. And then it was off to the toilet to throw up. With arms draped around the bowl, my head resting against one arm (a familiar position in the mornings), I lay there and retched for what must have been half an hour, until trickles of blood, mixed in with slivers of vomit, dripped from my mouth.

Not realising how much noise I was making, I heard a gentle knock at the door.

"Peter!" my sister called. "Are you all right?"

"Yeah, I'm okay. I won't be long."

The truth is I'd been retching like that most mornings for the best part of two years and had grown quite used to it. In fact, it had become something I took great comfort in. Now, this may sound rather strange, but the everyday pressures of my life were quite often much easier to face once I'd riven my guts up over a toilet bowl for at least half an hour every morning.

I think deep down I always kind of hoped that something would happen to me while I was being sick, and that would be it. I would be rushed off to hospital, given some sort of emergency treatment and then locked away in a secure unit somewhere until my system was finally clear of all that contaminated it. But, retch as I might, that never, ever happened, no matter how hard I tried. Yes, there was always another day to face, although it was much easier to do that knowing I had done my best to resist it. The glamorous lifestyle of a cocaine-dealing crack addict!

Vera was in the living room drinking a coffee by the time I appeared.

"Morning, Peter, go and help yourself to whatever you want – porridge, toast, eggs, whatever," she said, studying my face.

The mere mention of food would normally have been enough to send me running back to the toilet again, but I managed to fight off the temptation. I grimaced and shook my head. "Thanks, but no, I won't bother."

"Right, Peter, I have a few things I want to say to you, so sit down and pay attention."

Vera suddenly looked more serious than I had ever seen her, which at that time of day, without a drink in me, was somewhat disconcerting.

"Look, I've spoken to a few people, some friends and some family, and the general opinion is that I should turn you away, send you up to the hospital or something. But I've been thinking long and hard about what you said last night, and I've decided ... I'm not going to turn you away. I will try to help you if I can."

At that moment I realised that my sister was the only person in this world who cared enough for my welfare to actually try to help me.

"Do you understand what I'm saying?" she said, finally.

"Yeah," I said. "I do."

"Right, then, that's settled, although I will have to okay it with Emma and Andrea first," she said, her tone becoming lighter. Andrea, the eldest of her two daughters, was home from university and sleeping in the spare room, which meant I would have to stay on the sofa.

"Now, if you want a shower, go and help yourself to a towel. There's plenty of stuff in there for you to use, and once you've got yourself ready, and you feel up to it, we're going to visit Mum!"

Oh, yeah ... Mum! I thought. I had almost forgotten about her.

* * *

King Eric House, where my mother lived, is a care home in the middle of Lerwick made up of small, one-person apartments. It was purpose built in the 1980s to accommodate elderly people who are no longer able to live at home alone, but with minimal supervision they can maintain a certain degree of independence.

My mother, from what Vera told me, was very much borderline, and with the rate that the dementia was setting in, it wasn't known how much longer she would be able to stay there before being moved to a more specialised unit.

We entered her apartment and found her sitting alone.

"Hello, Mam!" Vera chirped happily. "How are you today? Are you fine?"

She looked round to see who it was, and already I could see a massive change in her. She just looked so vulnerable, afraid even, which certainly wasn't the mother I remembered.

"Oh, I'm not too bad," she replied, laughing a little. "Well, I've been a lot worse!"

"That's awful good to hear," Vera said, hanging our coats behind the door. "Look, I've brought somebody to see you."

My mother looked around once more.

"Do you know who this is?" Vera prompted.

"Oh, yes, yes ..." she said, looking interested.

"It's wir Peter!" Vera announced, flamboyantly.

"Yes, yes, of course, it is! It's Peter!" she exclaimed, her face lighting up.

My mother, although giving the impression she knew who I was, had no idea at all, that much was obvious. She had just become a little fly over the years concerning her mental degeneration, and this was how she had learned to respond under these circumstances. Having known for some time that she was ill, and what the prospects were, she had simply learned to answer questions in a way that would hopefully give the questioner the impression that she wasn't as ill as was made out.

It pulled at my heartstrings to see my mother trying so hard to execute this well-honed survival technique, which to be perfectly honest only revealed how ill she'd become.

Vera made us all some coffee and we sat there, just the three of us, talking and laughing and generally having a very pleasant time together until, after about an hour had passed, Vera announced that it was time for her to go to work a shift at the folk festival.

"So what are you going to do this afternoon, then?" she asked me.

It was only one o'clock and my sister was going off to work for the greatest part of the day, and possibly well into the early hours of the following morning. I glanced at my mother who was showing signs of confusion at Vera's departure.

"I don't know. I might give Brian a call to see what he's up to. I might as well let him know I'm back in Shetland."

Vera pulled her hand out of her bag and handed me a £20 note.

"Well, you just do whatever you need to do. I'll be home for a couple of hours in the evening, around five or six, so I'll hopefully see you then."

She said goodbye to our mother and left. Not sure what to do, I decided to stay with Mam a while longer. I made us more coffee and sat down next to her, but without Vera's presence in the room she was becoming increasingly anxious. She kept looking at the door, wondering where my sister had gone – not that she knew who Vera was.

I tried my best to talk with her, reassure her, perhaps, but she just wasn't able to communicate with me in quite the same way as my sister, making me feel rather inadequate. I could see just how much the Alzheimer's was affecting her. Although physically she was as healthy as I had ever known her, mentally she was a mere shadow of her former self.

Sensing how frightened she was becoming and realising how unable I was to deal with it, I told her to sit tight on the sofa and I made a quick exit. Feeling a little guilty, I found a member of staff and informed them of her increasing anxiety, and headed off as fast as I could in the direction of the nearest pub. Sadly, it was all I could think to do.

* * *

Sitting there in the depths of the Thule Bar, what I had just witnessed wouldn't leave me. In fact, my mind was going into overdrive thinking about my poor, old mother and how ill she had become. I also thought about my sister and what she must have had to cope with all those years, as our mother grew steadily worse. And I thought about myself, and what I had contributed, and was really very ashamed.

Yes, I felt like dirt sitting there in the bar that afternoon. My life hadn't been at all honouring to any of my family, and yet here I was, back in Shetland once more, vying for their sympathy and support.

What am I playing at? Who am I trying to bloody kid?

I began to question myself, searching my heart for answers, but everything that came back at me was negative, almost condemning.

Am I really doing the right thing? Can this really work? Can I really burden my sister with all this?

Vera, it was obvious, had enough to deal with without having my troubles laid onto her, too, but I honestly had nowhere else to turn. Yes, *my* troubles, always bloody me.

I just wasn't sure about anything anymore. I wasn't sure about being back in Shetland, and I certainly wasn't sure about me.

Am I even being sincere with her? Am I determined enough to go through with this? Is this really *what I want to do?*

Those were some of the more honest questions I asked myself. Did I, deep down inside, really want to change? That was what it would all come down to. Did I *really* want to change, or was I looking for a quick fix to my problems and a possible way out?

So many questions, and I honestly didn't know what to make of any of them. Finally, after a couple of hours sitting in a bar drinking, tormenting myself, doubting myself, judging myself, I eventually came to some kind of conclusion.

Look, Peter, whether or not you are being honest about wanting to do this, even if you don't think you have the conviction, can you not at least try? Can you not at least attempt to do this for your mother, who you've never done anything worthwhile for in your entire life? Can you not just try to do it for your father, who you made a promise to years ago, as he lay dying in hospital?

Yes, Peter, forget about whether you think you can or can't do it, and for once in your life think about them instead. Can you do it for them, Peter? And even if you think it doesn't matter, because they're no longer able to witness it, can you not do it for your sister, the only person in this world who genuinely cares about you?

Yes, I could – or at least, I hoped so.

* * *

That first weekend passed by in a bit of a blur. Vera would give me money each day to do whatever I needed to do to get through it, and in the evenings she would take me home a little carryout of beer. But her plan wasn't for it to carry on like that – which did seem a bit of a shame really, thoughts of my time with Catherine instantly springing to mind – as first thing on Monday morning Vera had something else in mind.

I remember her coming through into the living room at about 8 a.m., with this air of authority in her voice. She was most definitely more focused than she had been over the weekend and extremely determined, with a concrete plan all laid out for the way ahead.

The first thing she was going to do was to call CADSS (Community Alcohol & Drugs Services Shetland) and ask them to send someone along to the flat to see me. Nothing else, as far as she was concerned, would be acceptable. I was then instructed, in no uncertain terms, that I wasn't to leave the house, unless it was to attend any meetings that had been lined up for me, and I certainly wasn't to get too drunk, either! Having established the ground rules, Vera then went off to her work (the festival having finished, Islesburgh was back to being a community café once again), and I was left at home with Emma, who had instructions to keep a close eye on me.

About an hour must have passed – an hour in which Emma tried with great enthusiasm to get me to actually eat something – before the phone finally rang and Vera informed us that someone would be calling to arrange an appointment.

Glad that we knew what was happening at last, Emma and I then sat around watching television, glancing over at the clock every now and then in anticipation of this all-important phone call. But as morning approached mid-day and then slowly became mid-afternoon, with absolutely no sign of anyone attempting to make contact with me, Emma decided she had better call her mother and let her know.

Within as little as ten minutes of that call, Vera sent word back to us that she'd arranged a meeting with CADSS at their main office for four-thirty that afternoon.

Most annoyed that they hadn't done what they'd said they would, and even more annoyed when they tried to delay the meeting until Thursday (treatment dispensing day), Vera simply wouldn't give up, and perhaps sensing just how desperate she was, they agreed to squeeze us in.

A little while later, I met Vera outside the CADSS office and we walked in together. It kind of reminded me of when I was a little boy and my big sister had to take me places, just to make sure I went.

Once inside, Vera explained who she was and why we were there, then after a brief discussion with one or two drug councillors I was led away for an interview that seemed to take an eternity. To this day I have no idea what was said at that meeting, other than that an appointment was made for me to see a doctor on Wednesday, which was something I really looked forward to.

When I eventually arrived home from that meeting, Vera informed me – much to her amusement – that as I was interviewed she, too, had received counselling. She wouldn't share with me what had been discussed, but I remember her standing there in the kitchen, laughing.

"Yeah, yeah, I go along for you to get counselling and I end up getting it, too. Maybe I should've done it years ago!" she said, chortling away over a pan of boiling tatties.

One thing I loved about my sister was that she could always see the funny side of everything, which was probably just as well, having me as a little brother. It was so good to see her laughing, and I believe that laughter caused something to happen between us. It was as if an invisible wall, built up over many years – a wall of disappointment and heartache – had finally been broken down. From that moment on everything seemed to just flow.

Now, I can't recall every detail of what happened after that, or what my deepest thoughts were at the time, as it all happened so quickly, but it seemed almost effortless how it all pieced together, like some magical jigsaw.

WEDNESDAY 3 MAY

I saw the doctor and we discussed my addictions, as well as my physical health. It was obvious to everyone that I wasn't well. I was grossly underweight at 9¾ stone; I had a definite yellow complexion; my face looked sunken and my eye sockets were darkened. I was scruffy in appearance and lacked good hygiene, which I think was caused mostly by anxiety. I was constantly worrying about Aberdeen, Itchy and Scratchy, my sister ... I worried about anything and everything, all day long, which meant that a lot of important stuff, like having a wash or looking presentable, were added pressures I could do without.

The doctor took blood samples to run a blood/liver count and asked if I wanted to check for hepatitis C and HIV. Again I wanted to say "No", but instead I fought against it, pushing myself to finally accept responsibility over those troublesome issues, and at last I consented. Yes, it was finally time to face it, whether I liked it or not.

The doctor finished his examination and informed CADSS of his recommendations: that they put me onto a detox programme as soon as possible.

THURSDAY 4 MAY

Within 24 hours of the doctor's recommendation, I was at another meeting with a drug councillor. I was quickly assessed and given the go-ahead to take the next step, and an appointment was made for me at the Lerwick Health Centre on Friday afternoon, where I would be assessed again by a "drug nurse" for suitability.

FRIDAY 5 MAY

At the Health Centre I was met by a rather attractive nurse, who told me that she would be in charge of my programme and that I would be seeing quite a lot of her – which made me think this "detox thingy" might not be so bad, after all! She studied my notes and then, after talking some more about my health issues, agreed that I was, indeed, a suitable candidate for their regime.

I was then informed that I was going onto a seven-day detox, starting on Sunday night at eight o'clock, which I must admit came as something of a shock! I just hadn't expected it to begin so soon. However, this shock was quickly alleviated when she said that she would be coming to visit me at my sister's every morning to check my vital statistics.

Because they had no way of knowing how I would react initially, they would begin with a high dosage of a drug called Librium and monitor me closely to make sure that there were no adverse effects. So, with that in mind, it didn't seem quite so bad.

FRIDAY 5 – SATURDAY 6 MAY

On Friday night and all day Saturday, I went out drinking, this being my last weekend of freedom and all that. But I actually found that I was a lot more restrained than normal, and quite well-behaved, which was a surprise to everyone, including me! I met in with some old friends, even opening up to them about what I was in the process of doing, and yet another surprise was how supportive they all seemed to be.

SUNDAY 7 MAY

I had been in the bar all day with one or two old friends and eventually headed home for the allotted time. Vera waited patiently for my return, but the nearer the clock moved towards eight o'clock, the more nervous she became. Knowing I had gone out to meet some friends, who had planned a "send-off" drink, she worried that I might go over the top and not come back at all. But at five past eight I walked in to her apartment and plunked myself down on her sofa.

"So, I suppose that's that, then," I said, quite calmly.

Vera just looked at me and asked if I was going to drink any more that night, and although I really, really wanted to, I pushed it out of my mind and drank a cup of tea instead.

MONDAY 8 MAY

At approximately 8.30 a.m., Kathy, the "drug nurse", came to the house as promised. She did a blood test and found that my blood count was extremely low. I argued that I hadn't had a drink for over twelve hours and was so incensed that I even had her check my niece, who was lying on the other sofa, still drunk from the night before.

Andrea had come in blazing at around 2 a.m., deliberately waking me up in the process. She'd then lain down on the other sofa and spoken nonsense to me until thankfully falling asleep. About two hours later, I had wakened to the sound of a crashing thump as she rolled off the sofa in her sleep and onto the floor. I'd grudgingly had to rise and lift her back on to it, which hadn't been easy.

Andrea agreed to the test, purely for the fun of it, but her result was fine, which I found quite incredible!

"After the state she was in last night?" I exclaimed.

Kathy explained that the difference between the two results was probably due to the fact that I had been drinking every day over a longer period of time.

Hmm, she obviously doesn't know Andrea! I thought. But who was I to argue? The results spoke for themselves.

Andrea's in the clear and you're not. End of story, PJ. But if Andrea's in the clear and you're not, then you really must be in trouble!

* * *

The seven-day detox went remarkably well. I started taking my pills that Monday morning and was surprised at how focused I was, feeling somehow very different inside. It was as if I could feed on the challenge set before me and that, in turn, gave me some sort of power over it. It certainly wasn't like anything I had experienced before; such positivity wasn't like me.

But, then, I also had the support of my lifelong friend, Brian. He would call me quite regularly and take me out fishing, or for runs in his car, just the two of us, out into the country somewhere. Brian also owned a rather lovely croft house, which he thought required whitewashing, so taking advantage of my predicament he had me out there working.

It was a lovely spring that year, with the sun shining down every day of my detox, and as I painted, fished and drove around the island with Brian, I could feel myself being re-energised by the sun's rays. I was tanning on the outside, and it almost felt like I was tanning on the inside, too. Within three days of the programme beginning, I was truly feeling like a new man, something Brian was also aware of.

I remember standing beside him one particular afternoon, as we worked at his house, just talking away as usual as he tried to fix some piece of machinery. I suddenly realised that he had stopped what he was doing and was just sitting there looking up at me and laughing.

"What? What are you laughing at?" I asked him, suddenly self-conscious.

"Peter," he replied, "I'm not laughing at you. It's just so good to see you looking so happy!"

I then realised that Brian was right; I was genuinely happy. And when I thought a little more about what he'd just said, I knew at that moment I was probably the happiest I had been in my entire life. I will never forget that feeling.

Of course, not everything was fun and games at that time, as there were other issues at hand. Kathy, for instance, had mentioned to Vera that I really needed to consider going into rehab once the detox was over. She mentioned the name of one establishment here in Shetland called the Papa Stour Project, a facility for supporting young men with addiction problems, situated on a small island off the west coast of Shetland.

This was actually the second time it had been mentioned to me. The first I had heard about it was from an old friend, Aaron Irvine, who I had bumped into one afternoon in the Thule Bar, on the same day, in fact, that I had made the rather hasty exit from my mother's home.

Aaron, who had his own problems with addiction, had already spent some time there and although he had relapsed, he thought it might "do me the world of good". I never really took on board much of what he said about his time there, as it wasn't something I thought I would ever consider, but as Kathy brought up the subject once more, and my sister had a hold of the idea, well, I knew it wasn't going to go away in a hurry. It was something that would be mentioned time and time again.

Then, at an appointment with the doctor to hear the results of those blood tests, it turned out that although my blood count was fine, the liver function test showed a problem. The count was extremely high, somewhere around the 700 mark, and when you consider that a normal, healthy liver should read somewhere between five and 32, then as the doctor remarked, "Seven hundred is not very good, no."

To be honest, I hadn't expected to hear anything else; in fact, it was probably much better than I imagined it would be.

And, once again, Papa Stour was mentioned.

"The thing to do, Peter, is not worry too much about it. It's not like it can't be reversed," the doctor encouraged. "Now, if you were to consider going to the rehab, even for as little as a month, as you have cited as a possibility, then when you come out we can run another test to see whether the count has come down or not. If it has come down, then that's great, but if it hasn't, then we'll have another look at what's going on. But, please, don't go away from here worrying about it, not just yet, anyway."

Straight after that meeting, I went along to Vera's work and told her what the doctor had said.

"Oh, Peter, I really think you should listen to us. Look, it's Friday, and you're already five days into the treatment. Kathy told me just how encouraged she is by your attitude towards it all. She thinks you're doing extremely well. Please, will you think about going to Papa Stour?"

It was certainly a lot to consider, almost too much to take in, and I couldn't be sure what to do for the best. A little later I mentioned it to Brian, seeking his opinion.

"Papa Stour, eh?" he said, sounding impressed. "You should definitely go!"

"What makes you say that?" I asked, thinking he would have something deep and meaningful for me to consider.

"Because it's the only island in Shetland I haven't been to yet," he replied. "Just go! Okay?"

Not fully convinced by Brian's line of reasoning, I now at least had the opinions of everyone who mattered to me.

Kathy, who I had taken quite a shine to, thought I should go; my doctor, who I was very impressed by and had developed a lot of respect for, thought that I should go; my sister, who had already done so much for me, and wanted nothing more than to see me well again, thought that I should go; and my good friend, Brian, who had never been there before, but thought that was as good a reason for me to go as any, thought I should go.

I must admit, even taking in to consideration the opinions of everyone who mattered to me, I still didn't know what to do for the best, until I was reminded of exactly where this island lay and that I actually had a relationship with it that went much deeper than those who were trying to push it onto me realised.

* * *

It was Sunday, 14 May. Vera had taken Mam around to her flat for dinner, which was something she had decided to do every Sunday she was available, and hoped to keep doing for as long as my mother was able. It was also nearing the end of my detox and whatever lay ahead, and so it was a celebration of sorts.

I sat there with my sister and her two daughters, my mother next to me, and although she wasn't anything like she used to be, it was just like being a family again. There I was, sitting with the people who mattered most in this world, and I was just so thankful for the time together. I knew that things could have been so very different.

Looking around the room at everyone there, I knew just how lucky I was to have such wonderful people who were taking so much time out of their lives to try to help me in mine.

Yes, I owed it to them, and almost everyone else I had come into contact with since returning to Shetland, but most of all I owed it to me.

Monday morning, May 15, saw the end of my detox, and on Wednesday, 17 May, at four in the afternoon, I was whisked off to Papa Stour.

CHAPTER 9

Papa Stour is a very small island situated a mile or two off the west coast of Shetland, with a population of around 14 people, who are mostly just enjoying their retirement, doing a little crofting or fishing on the side maybe, but in general just living very quiet, almost reclusive lives. There are no shops or public amenities to speak of and the school has closed.

When I arrived, the island's only B & B no longer operated, and even the one public telephone appeared to have been removed from its box. As far as I could tell, the only thing that could be construed as a legitimate business was a Christian-run rehabilitation centre for drug addicts called the Papa Stour Project. Not what you would expect, really.

Now, much as I didn't like the idea of being stuck on "Papatraz" for a whole day, never mind a whole month, I also struggled with how far away it was from civilisation – about an hour's drive west of Lerwick, and then another 45 minutes by ferry. On top of that, there was – in my view, anyway – a distinct lack of 21st Century facilities. There was, however, an incentive for me to go there that no one other than my sister was really aware of. You see, directly across the sea from Papa Stour, approximately one mile away on the mainland, sits the only other community for absolutely miles around: the little village of Sandness.

Admittedly, I hadn't been overly enthused to begin with about going there, but I was very aware of what lay close to Papa Stour's shores, and held this romantic idea of each day being able to go off on my own, perhaps, to look out over the very village where my father had been born and raised. But why should that have made a difference to me? I mean, it wasn't as if Sandness had ever been a part of my life, or was even spoken of by my father. Nevertheless, it was a part of my history and who I was, and that was something I was deeply interested in.

When the decision was finally taken to go to Papa Stour, I was reminded of the last time I saw my father and was instantly back at that place again.

* * *

My father's run of poor health finally took its toll on him and in May 1999, at the Gilbert Bain Hospital in Lerwick, he lay dying of cancer. By then I had virtually lost all contact with my family. I was 31 years old, had been living in Aberdeen for almost ten years, and was a complete and utter cocaine addict with an intravenous habit of between 2 – 5 g per day.

My sister and brother had been doing their absolute best to look after my father as his health deteriorated, and were also coping with my mother, who was by then showing signs of having some form of dementia. During this time I was busy working with gangsters from Liverpool, fast becoming one of the biggest cocaine dealers in Aberdeen city centre, and was oblivious to all they were going through. I had lost touch with reality, let alone the struggles of home.

My sister, it turned out, had been trying to contact me for weeks, months even, to let me know what had been happening concerning my parents, but I had disappeared off the radar completely. There was no record of me holding an address, receiving social security benefits or paying taxes. None of my old friends in Shetland seemed able to help either, and the more people she contacted concerning my whereabouts, the less chance she was given of finding me.

Leading up to those final days, and causing her many a sleepless night, Vera worried that I would miss the opportunity to see my father before he passed away, but through blind determination on her part, and a fluke call to a bar on Aberdeen's Union Street, her message miraculously managed to find its way to me, with what turned out to be days to go. I called her as soon as I heard that she was searching for me, and immediately booked myself on the overnight ferry back to Shetland.

I arrived in Lerwick the following morning and went straight to my mother's, where I met up with my sister. She briefly filled me in on the current situation regarding my father, especially about what to expect. According to Vera my father was barely conscious, a shadow of the man he once was and quite delirious a lot of the time. She also told me not to be upset if he didn't know who I was, which saddened me, but later that morning, as we walked into his hospital room – already occupied by two of his sisters – he looked quite awake and alert, surprising us both.

Vera watched me as I approached his bedside, trying to gauge my reactions, but all I could do was smile, this big, happy feeling welling up inside me, as our eyes finally met after what felt like a very long time.

"Do you know who this is that's come to see you, Dad?" Vera asked him, softly.

He looked up at me and then completely astonished everyone.

"Yes," he said, smiling back at me, "it's Peter!"

I sat down next to him and tried talking with him, but we didn't have a chance to say a great deal; there was too much going on around us, or at least that's what I told myself. The truth was that we simply didn't know how to communicate with one another, which was made all the harder under these very difficult circumstances.

Throughout the rest of that day I didn't venture far from the room, only ever popping out for something to eat and – when possible – to cram as much drink and drugs into my system as I could. It was a shameful thing to be doing at such a time, and very clearly upsetting to my family, but I couldn't help myself. I was an alcoholic, a drug addict; what else could I do?

The following morning, however, I was back up at his room early and this time we were alone. I sat there holding his hand, hoping he would open his eyes so that we might have a chance to speak, but he didn't. It was, perhaps, just as well, as we would never have known what to say to one another.

And so, in my mind, I began to say all the things I'd really hoped I could say to his face, bringing tears to my eyes.

I'm so sorry, Dad, for all the trouble I've caused you. I'm so sorry I have always been such a let-down to you. I didn't mean to make you ill and I never meant to hurt you ...

My thoughts went on and on, as my heart kept breaking, and as I sat there looking sorrowfully at his white and sunken face, I was suddenly reminded of another time my father and I were in such close proximity, just the two of us. It had been one of only about half a dozen such occasions, between the ages of nine and 12 years old ...

* * *

My mother and father always liked to go out for a drink at the weekends, and having a child this late in their lives certainly wasn't going to stop them. I had absolutely no problem with them going out all the time; in fact, I used to enjoy it just as much, if not more, than they did, because that meant finding someone to look after me, and more often than not that someone was my cousin, Jenny.

Jenny, who was around 15 or 16 at the time, was by far my favourite babysitter. She was good fun and quite pretty really, and would always have a right carry on, bringing with her a few of her friends. She also had a younger brother and sister, who were more my own age, who would often come along and we'd all have a great time together. While Jenny and her friends would sneak drink from my mother's booze cabinet, we younger ones did whatever we pleased.

One night, however, Jenny had to cancel and because they were unable find a replacement babysitter at such short notice, she sent along a slightly older, male friend of hers. I came home about eight o'clock in the evening to find this strange man sitting on our sofa, and then a few minutes later I suddenly found myself alone there with him.

A little later in the evening – I can't be at all sure of the time, and I can't quite recall how it happened – he took a hold of me and sexually assaulted me in the middle of our living room. He had a hold of me and had my trousers down, doing stuff that I didn't want him to, and he wouldn't let me go. I remember being extremely frightened. Shortly after that it all becomes rather vague. There was a lot of rubbing against me and touching, and then I saw his manhood in his hand. I don't seem to remember any more after that. All recollection seems to cease, although I don't know why. I don't know how it ended or what must have happened to bring it to an end – and in many ways I hope I never do.

The thing is, I never told my parents what happened that night; in fact, I never told anyone. I knew that it would only hurt them and there would be a lot of trouble to follow – as if I didn't cause them enough difficulty as it was! I also feared greatly for my father's health and how this would affect him if he knew. All that I could realistically do was ask them never to have him round again, which seemed more than fair enough to me.

"If you can't get Jenny, then don't get anyone, certainly not that guy you had last time!" I said to them one evening shortly after, as they began making plans to go out.

Well, like everything I voiced, it simply fell on deaf ears, as a couple of weeks later there he was again, sitting on our sofa with that same shifty look in his eyes. I didn't say anything; my parents just looked so happy to be going out, and so all I could do was promise myself that he wouldn't do it to me again, but, of course, he did.

The following weekend they were looking for yet another babysitter (Jenny was supposedly seeing another new boyfriend and didn't have time for babysitting any more), and so I listened carefully to the names of possible candidates.

"Look, if you can't get Jenny, then I don't want anyone!" I told my mother.

They just ignored me and so I started to lay it on, becoming really difficult, extremely angry even, almost to the point of screaming at them, until finally Mam gave in and made the decision that my father would just have to stay at home with me instead! My mum then went off to wherever she was going and my dad just sat there in his usual chair, drinking his beer and whisky, never a word coming from his mouth.

I will never forget that night and how I sat at his feet, looking up at him every now and then as I amused myself on the floor. I remember wondering what kind of stuff he thought about as he sat there, humming along to his favourite records, drinking his drinks and smoking the odd fag, which incidentally, he would only ever do in front of me. Never once did he try to talk to me, or for that matter did I try speaking to him. I just sat there on the carpet, sorting through my old stamp collection, hoping that he might show some interest in it, but he was a million miles away, listening to Englebert Humperdinck laying off about some woman's "Spanish Eyes".

I really wished then that I had the courage to tell him what had happened to me, and the real reason why he'd had to stay at home with me that night. I was frightened, confused, and desperate for someone to put their arms around me and tell me that nothing like that would ever happen to me again. But I didn't say a thing; I just didn't want to hurt them or cause any more upset than I already had. I had simply been the cause of so much distress in our family and was frightened of what this would do, and so my lips remained sealed.

* * *

Sitting by his bedside in that hospital room years later certainly brought back many a memory, some good, some bad, but none of them really reflected our true relationship.

As a child, the connection we had was something I never really understood. A part of me simply grew up believing that I had been the cause of so much grief in his life – so much so that it had affected his very health – and whatever we lacked as father and son had been my fault.

Now, sitting at his side, I found myself finally able to make sense of it all, ready to accept responsibility for it, but at the same time, I knew that after all those years, it was much too late to do the one thing I really wanted to do. He would never hear me say how sorry I was, and I would never have his forgiveness.

However, there was one major breakthrough in amongst the myriad of memories and tangled emotions, as I was finally able to accept who he was.

All my life I had tried not to be like my father. It's a sorry thing to admit, but it's true. I hated the way he never stood up to my mum; I hated the way he was always ill; I hated the way he never seemed to be much fun at parties; I hated the way we never talked; I just hated so much about the way he was. But, having said all that, I always loved him. I just never wanted to be like him.

In some respects I became the person I did because of that, and the thing that drove me to despair throughout it all was that no matter how hard I had tried not to become like him, I could see it happening more and more each day, with every look in the mirror and with every cough from my smoke-damaged lungs.

Until, all of a sudden, sitting there in that hospital room – catching the odd glimpse of the man who was my father in between brief spells of consciousness and hallucination – I saw something that made me very proud to be his son.

You see, all my life I had been running from myself, drinking away the thought that I might one day be like him, and injecting drugs with the hope that day would never come. But in the blink of an eye I could see, lying there before me, and so very sadly dying, someone who was – and always had been – ten times the man I was or could ever hope to be.

There was I, working the drugs and crime in Aberdeen, running with gangsters, with people of extreme violence, and thinking this made me someone. It was earning me the respect that my father never had (or so I thought), that I wouldn't otherwise have. But, as I sat there, my arms and wrists throbbing from injecting, a man completely resigned to the utter seediness and true depravation of what his life had become, I was suddenly filled with the greatest conviction and a feeling that tore the very heart from me.

Who was I to think that my father was any less of a man, just because he never lost his temper or acted the fool when he was on the booze? Who was I to have been so ashamed of a man who had only ever tried to do his best for those he loved? Who was I to have thought he was weak, when he had struggled all his life and never once complained about it?

He had done everything that a kind, honest, loving man could do. He had worked all his days, even through ill health, to give us a decent home, holidays every year, great presents at Christmas, pocket money every day – and he never once grumbled or complained; he just very simply did everything that was expected of a loving father and husband, and he did so very humbly.

I held his hand, as cold as it had become, as frail as it felt to my touch, and told him there and then, in the quiet of that hospital room: "Dad, I promise you that one day I will get free of all of this, and I will do it for you, and just so you know ... I love you, and I'm sorry for everything that I have put you through!"

I had no way of knowing if he could hear me or not, but something inside told me that he could.

My father died a while later, at around 1 o'clock in the morning, and was buried a few days later on a Tuesday afternoon.

But it wasn't just my father that died that day; buried along with him was the hope that he would one day see me as someone he could actually be proud of. All I would be left with was the bitterness of regret.

Papa Stour, I hoped, would be a place where I could confront the guilt I had been carrying for so long, and somehow leave it behind.

* * *

To begin with I found the whole island thing a bit much. The ferry that serviced the island, I discovered on arrival, only ran on certain days of the week, and although there were flights on and off Papa Stour, they were even less frequent, and so there quickly followed this feeling of isolation, which I didn't really like.

It probably didn't help matters that I was the only Scottish person at North House (the rehab). Not that I'm a racist, or have any problems with people of another tongue, but in my experience being surrounded by Englishmen could at times be a little disconcerting. Andy and Sabina, who owned and managed the rehab, were a couple of friendly, ageing and quite eccentric hippies, who had moved to Shetland during the early Seventies after being kicked out of a hippy commune for deciding to practice monogamy. And then there was John, a drug support worker, who was undoubtedly as Cockney as any East Londoner I had ever met, and someone who, I will admit, I found to be something of an oddity.

John just wasn't the kind of man I expected to find working in a Christian rehab. For instance, he had a long goatee beard and a skinhead haircut; he also had tattoos up and down both arms, one of which was a fading "West Ham", with a couple of crossed-over hammers hovering threateningly below it. He was an extremely stocky lad, too, quite the hard man really, with what looked very much like the scars of a violent past etched into the side of his face. He'd seemed friendly enough when I'd first made his acquaintance, albeit briefly at the CAADS offices in Lerwick a week before, but it felt like a different story being stuck on a small island with him. And so, even though I was the only native in that environment, I felt extremely out of place and at times a little insecure!

Right from the word go, and certainly during those first couple of days, I struggled desperately with being there. It wasn't so much the Englishness of North House, as I didn't have that much of a problem with it, although it did sometimes make me feel a little like an outsider; no, what unsettled me more than anything was what was expected of me.

The very first evening I arrived, from having my bags and person searched (by John, no less), to having to sit with everyone at a dining table as we ate dinner, make conversation and try to look interested in what they were saying, to even having to help with the dishes afterwards ... Well, I just wasn't prepared for all the closeness. I felt totally hemmed in, which set me off on the wrong footing altogether. But grumble to myself as I might, I quickly realised that I didn't have much choice in the matter, and that being sociable, as well as fitting in to routines, was what was expected of me for the next 30 days!

I hated the concept of routines and endless instructions, but that's exactly what I was given. I had to rise at six-thirty in the morning and have a shower, then because it was lambing season, I was to check on the ewes and give the expectant mothers some added nutrition in the form of ewe nuts and look to see if there were any new arrivals and report my findings to Andy. Then I had to let the chickens out of the coop and collect in all the eggs.

On re-entering the house, I would have time for a quick wash and then at 8 a.m. I would join the others for morning worship and prayer time. Once that was finished, we would all have a little breakfast and then I was expected to help clear the table and wash the dishes. When all that was over, the real work would begin and I would go off out with Andy to do a little "eco therapy": fix fences, dig ditches, move sheep from one field to another, and so on.

After an hour or so, we would have yet another food break, clear the table, do more dishes, then go back out to work some more around the croft, planting vegetables or building dry stone walls, until I was absolutely knackered – there just seemed to be no end to it! To say that I wasn't physically up to the task would be an understatement! But I wasn't one to give in easily and although I had to constantly push myself, almost to the point of breaking, I seemed to get through whatever was expected of me.

There was one task, however, on top of everything else, which I really took umbrage with. It was nothing more strenuous than a certain workbook, *Life Shapers*, which I was to attend to during my "personal study time". A workbook designed to help the user examine himself/herself mentally, emotionally and spiritually, it is meant to be a three-month course consisting of 12 weekly studies. Each study comprises a list of daily questions that help you delve into all aspects of "Who You Think Are", with the aim of bringing you to some kind of understanding of yourself, and ultimately what lies at the root of your problems.

I remember lying awake at night and wondering what on earth I had let myself in for. The work was, at times, quite hard – well, it was to someone like me – and I hated being told what to do. But what was the alternative? Cirrhosis of the liver? Aberdeen? Itchy and Scratchy? No, I knew what I was there for, and that I needed to try to stick it out as best I could, but that decision certainly wasn't made any easier with the introduction of that workbook.

As helpful as the others considered it, I utterly despised that book! From the moment it was handed to me and explained with great enthusiasm, I wanted nothing at all to do with it, especially when informed that I wouldn't have the normal week to settle in first, and was expected to press on with immediate effect. (Usually the client would be given a week to settle in before beginning *Life Shapers*, however, because I had only agreed to spend a month at North House – a month being my one and only condition – the routine had been altered and I was put straight on to the workbooks without delay.) I was simply handed a Bible

– the Project was Christian at its core, and the workbooks involved the reading of Biblical Scripture – and more or less told to go and get on with it.

I will never forget taking the workbook to my room and looking through the list of questions for day one, with the intention of at least trying, and then launching it into the corner. Funnily enough, the same thing happened the following morning, and again later that evening; in fact, it seemed to happen every time I picked it up. I would look over the list of questions for that particular day, even ponder them a little, before this anger would rise up and the book would be thrown across my bedroom with utter contempt.

"What is this rubbish? I know fine well who and what I am! Just who do they think they are, expecting me to do this?" I would moan under my breath.

Yet, as much as I was unwilling to engage with the programme, I was somehow managing to read the Bible that had been given to me on the very first night I had arrived. Yes, I had felt distinctly excited about that, although not from a desire to learn about God or find out about His Son, Jesus, but rather the exact opposite. I was really only interested in what it had to say about the devil, the end of the world, and all that extremely interesting doomsday stuff. I remember asking, almost as soon as I held it in my hand, where I would find such information, and Andy recommending that I "avoid all that for the time being, and read the Gospel of John instead".

So, a little disappointed, that was what I tried to do. Late in the evening, or early in the morning, even during occasional quiet times throughout the day, I would read a chapter or two from John's Gospel, while at the same time trying to read another book that Sabina had recommended. *Chasing the Dragon* told the story of Jackie Pullinger's work among drug addicts in the Kowloon Walled City in Hong Kong. It was a story Sabina thought might encourage me, and so it was that *Life Shapers* didn't really have a look in.

* * *

After a few days had passed, I was managing a little better, having come to terms with life at North House. I was up really early in the morning, mostly because I wasn't sleeping very well at nights, and was outside doing my chores before anyone else had surfaced. I had developed an appetite for food that was beginning to put a little colour back into my yellowy cheeks; I was growing ever more appreciative of the solitude and quiet of Papa Stour; and I had made good friends with Ralph, a three-legged sheepdog, who would always join me on my little walks along the cliff tops, where we would sit together for long periods as I gazed out over Sandness, while feeling rather sorry for myself. I had also become "mother" to Pumpkin, a caddy lamb I would feed with a bottle at regular intervals throughout the day.

Against all the odds I was developing a reasonably good relationship with my carers, Andy, Sabina and, of course, John. Yes, it did all take a little getting used to at first, but I soon began to mellow.

However, there was still that nagging problem of *Life Shapers*. On the afternoon of day four, I still hadn't managed to write anything in it. The book itself was looking ever more ragged from occasional projectile trips across my bedroom, and was still every bit as offensive to me then as it had been the first time I looked at it. I probably had as much intention of filling it in then as when it was first handed to me.

I was upstairs in the clients' quarters having a few games of table tennis with John, during what had been allocated as personal study time, when Andy entered the room.

"So, Pete," he called over, as he made his way to the quiet area and sat down on one of the sofas, "how you getting on with that workbook we gave you?"

I'd just suffered a rather embarrassing defeat to John at the table tennis, so regardless of what Andy might have on his mind, I was happy to throw down the bat and join him.

“Truth is, Andy,” I replied, making my way across the room, “I just can’t get to grips with it. I just don’t think it’s for me.”

I really quite liked Andy. He had a great sense of humour and was very interesting to listen to. I spent quite a lot of my time with him, mostly working outside with the sheep and such like, as well as the odd spell throughout the day when he would join me in the quiet area and just speak about stuff; well, about Jesus mostly, but also about his time as an LSD-popping, pot-smoking hippy during 1960’s London, which was always very interesting and really quite amusing, too.

I slumped down in one of the armchairs across from him, studying his face a little, trying to work out where this conversation might be heading.

“How’s that then?’ he asked. ‘What are you finding so difficult about it?”

“Och, I don’t know,” I replied, cautiously. “I just can’t relate to what it’s asking me, Andy, it’s as simple as that, really. It’s irrelevant.”

A silence grew between us that quickly became a little uncomfortable, until I began feeling somewhat self-conscious. *Is he having a go at me here?* I thought. *Is he pushing this on me? He needn’t bother*.

And with that I went on the defensive.

“Well, look, it’s asking me stuff like: ‘How do you think other people see you?’” As if that was enough of an answer.

“Aha ...” Andy replied, rather smugly in my view.

“Well, to be honest with you, Andy, I couldn’t really care how anyone sees me; that’s just not a problem here.”

Andy said nothing. He scratched his chin a little and continued looking at me, obviously considering how best to deal with this situation. Not liking this cross-examination, and feeling I was in control, I just carried on.

“And that question: ‘How do you see yourself?’ Well, I have no problem there either, as I know fine well what I am. Yeah, I have issues, but who hasn’t? Look, I know I’ve made mistakes in life, but so what? Who hasn’t, eh?”

I could feel my face turn red as my blood began to boil, indicating – to me, at least – that I was verging on a familiar thing called "rant mode". And although I should have known better, having recognised what was about to happen, I carried on anyway, the momentum taking me past the point of no return.

"And as for that stupid question: 'How do you think God sees you?' Well, between you and me, Andy, eh, and no offence here, okay ..." By this time I was leaning over the coffee table, putting myself right in his face "... I don't think your God is particularly bothered, do you? I mean, He must have far greater things to worry about than me, like feeding all the starving kids in Africa, wouldn't you agree?"

I hadn't realised up until that point just how frustrated I was. I mean, I was mentally and physically unwell, and deep down I didn't particularly hold out much hope of this ever working. I was absolutely terrified; terrified at the thought of going back out into the world again; terrified at the thought of slipping back into my old ways; terrified of letting everyone down. I had major concerns, which I obviously didn't know how to voice.

I did become aware that going on at Andy was unfair, but I just couldn't help myself. I so needed to let off some steam, and not only because of my situation, but at the ridiculous notion that God was going to somehow solve everything for me.

"Look, Pete," Andy said, noticing how angry I had suddenly become, "you don't have to fill in that workbook if you don't want to. In fact, we should really have been working closer with you on it, so please don't let it get to you. It's our fault, Pete, not yours. We just haven't given you the proper time you need. Look, if it's any consolation, I'm really, really sorry for having laid that on you, okay?"

Just then, John, who I had forgotten was even in the room, offered his opinion. Standing against the table tennis table listening to our conversation, he had been quietly observing everything that was going on.

"Yeah, Andy's right, we should be giving you a lot more support. It's just that we haven't had anyone come here for as short a time as you before, and I suppose we weren't sure how to gauge it. It was kind of new to us, too, mate."

It was easy to see that Andy was actually deeply moved by my reaction and possibly a bit frightened, too, but I could tell he was genuinely sorry – not that it was an apology I was after.

I began to feel a little sorry for him, as well as embarrassed about my initial take on the conversation, and although I wasn't quite willing to apologise, I decided to change the subject.

"Look, I've been reading my Bible and I'm half way through that Gospel you told me to read," I told him, hoping this would put things onto a lighter footing.

John, sensing that things weren't going to get out of hand, left us alone as he needed to prepare the vegetables for the evening meal.

"Pete, that's fantastic!" Andy exclaimed, the tension visibly leaving him. "How are you finding it? I mean, are you enjoying it? Is it making much sense?"

It was good that he was able to smile again, and I felt a little better myself.

"Yeah, I suppose it is, but I'm a bit sceptical. I'm just not too sure about the whole Jesus thing. I mean, wasn't He just a man, at the end of the day?"

Andy sat there for a minute or two, obviously thinking through an answer.

"Do you believe in God, Pete?" he asked, eventually.

"Yeah, I suppose I do believe in God. I believe in life after death and all that, but what difference will that make?"

And so Andy began to explain to me about God; about His initial plan for mankind as depicted in the book of Genesis, chapter one; about the rebellion of satan and the consequential fall of Adam and Eve in the Garden of Eden and the need for a sacrifice to pay the penalty for man's disobedience. He then went on to explain how this all tied in with the coming of the Messiah, the life, death and resurrection of God's precious Son, Jesus – the only One worthy enough to pay that debt – and how the Salvation of our souls can only come through faith in Him.

I listened intently to what, I suppose, was my first ever sermon, and not only through politeness either, but through a genuine interest in this subject. You see, I did believe in the supernatural, I always had. The unfortunate thing for me was that I had always believed more in the forces of evil, believing them to have real power. After all, I had been witness to it on more than one occasion, especially as a result of one particular incident that, for some reason, came flooding back to me after so many years ...

* * *

It was a Saturday night and I was about nine years old; my parents had gone out to the pub and my cousin, Jenny, and her younger sister, Clare, had come to stay the night, as they quite often would when minding me.

As usual, shortly after my parents left Jenny's friends would all magically appear out of the woodwork. On this particular occasion, they seemed more excited than usual, and I discovered that they were planning to hold a séance.

I watched with much amusement as they cleared the coffee table and put down their board, turned a glass on its end in the middle, lit a few candles, opened a few bottles of wine and closed the curtains. It was all very exciting and I was really looking forward to it, until Jenny informed Clare and me that we weren't allowed to sit in on it and were instead to go and play outside until it was over.

About two hours later, the living room door suddenly burst open and all these teenage girls came running out into the hall with their coats in their hands, making as fast as they could for the front door. Out of curiosity I looked in to see Jenny doing a quick tidy up of the living room, before grabbing hold of Clare and me, and physically dragging us both upstairs and making us all climb into the one bed together.

Lying there in total confusion – Jenny tucked safely in the middle – she told us what had happened. It turned out that they had, indeed, managed to contact a spirit, but the spirit turned out to be an evil one. It was spelling stuff out on the board, horrible things about those sitting there, as strange things began to happen in the room. Then, out of sheer terror, someone knocked over the glass and everyone fled, but not before it had an opportunity to give one last message, and it was this: "If Peter tells anyone what happened here tonight, I will stay with him forever."

I remember being completely shocked at this revelation. I mean, why me? Why did it have to single *me* out? I hadn't even been allowed in the room!

At nine years old, I wasn't sure what to make of it. Was Jenny just saying that so I wouldn't tell my parents? It was possible, but Jenny should have known by then that I never told my parents anything, especially if there was a possibility that I might land her in trouble. But, it was either that or the only other alternative; it *had* really happened like she had said it had. Obviously, I couldn't be sure, so for a while I thought it best to stay safe and not say anything to anyone – until, perhaps a week or two later, when I confided in a friend at school.

I didn't give it much thought after that until the following weekend, when I came home to find the strange man who'd been drafted in to babysit sitting on our sofa. Jenny had suddenly decided that she couldn't do it anymore. Later that night, when we were alone and he sexually abused me, I distinctly remember the look in his eyes as he carried out the attack; there was something distinctly evil about them.

Ever since then I'd strongly believed in the supernatural. I believed I was being watched – haunted – especially in my own home, and that had strengthened this belief I already held, that I was somewhat evil inside. The countless number of times I had brought despair to my parents; the fact that I had made my father so ill; well, who could have done those things – especially from such a young age – other than someone who truly had been cursed? That was certainly what I believed and at times was made to believe.

* * *

Listening to Andy that afternoon on Papa Stour, I could tell that he truly believed every word he was saying, and I really admired him for that, but it also made me wonder ... If such a rational human being could wholeheartedly confess to believing in all this stuff, then surely there must be something in it ...

We sat there in silence once more, until eventually Andy spoke.

"Pete, Jesus is real, and so is His promise that if we ask Him into our hearts He will come and dwell within us, making us more like Him, with the help of the Holy Spirit. Pete, He can and *will* help you, if you will only let Him!"

I said nothing.

"Pete, would you like to trust your life to Christ?" Andy asked, rather awkwardly, it must be said. "Would you like to invite Him into your heart now? I mean, it's up to you, mate; I'm not trying to pressure you or anything like that. I just think it's something you should really consider, and well, He's here with us right now, waiting for you to call on Him."

I looked around the room a little suspiciously, half expecting John to come jumping up from behind one of the sofas, all dressed up in sackcloth and sandals, or something.

"Eh, okay, then," I replied. "I don't suppose it can do any harm, can it?"

"No, Pete, it most definitely cannot!"

I hesitated once more and then agreed.

"Okay, let's do it!"

Andy then asked a few questions: did I believe that Jesus was the true Son of God; did I willingly invite Him into my heart; was I willing to put my trust in Him and allow Him to work in my life and most importantly, did I recognise the need for His forgiveness and promise to turn from my ways and follow Him along whatever path my life may take?

To all of which I quite emphatically answered, "Yes."

Andy's face lit up like I had never seen it before and as he began to pray for me, committing my declaration of faith in Jesus to God the Father, on closing my eyes I saw something I found quite remarkable – a tear dropping from his.

* * *

Immediately following our prayer time, a few interesting things began to develop. I didn't feel drawn anymore to my little retreat, where I would gaze out over Sandness feeling sorry for myself. I began to read my Bible with a bit more zeal, looking back over various aspects of what Jesus taught, trying my hardest to understand it. I was coping better with the "no smoking" rule at North House – although I did still wear those nicotine patches and have one of those plastic cigarette filters constantly hanging from my mouth – and I started to feel a lot happier about myself, and much less of an outsider.

It was a massive turn around in just about every way possible. I was feeling a lot more positive, with this real sense of hope. But, as always seemed to be the case with me, the honeymoon period never lasted very long ...

A few days later, the excitement of what I had done had waned considerably and I began to have serious doubts about the whole thing. Had giving my life to Jesus really made any difference to me, or was it all in my mind?

I then began to believe that I'd probably been extremely foolish. I'd been foolish to believe what the Bible said about Jesus; foolish to believe that things could really change; foolish to believe that there was ever any real hope, and foolish to believe that God would want to help me. I even began to doubt the sincerity of the workers at the Project. My mind was in absolute turmoil, but I struggled on throughout that day, holding on, I suppose, to the hope that something more might yet happen.

Later that evening, I was up in the clients' lounge once more. John had just taken another scalp, this time on the pool table, and Sabina, who had come to see what we were up to, stood at the window watching a couple of love-sick otters frolicking along the shoreline, about a hundred yards below the house.

"So, Peter, how was your day?" she asked, leaving the window and walking across the room to one of the sofas in the quiet area. "How's Pumpkin doing? We're thinking that we'll have to move him into the field with the rams. He should be okay in there. He's a feisty little lad," she said, rather reflectively.

I stood watching from the window as the otters, suddenly aware of Ralph's clumsy attempt to sneak up on them, bobbed along the shoreline a little, as if to tease him before slipping smoothly out of sight beneath the gently lapping waves.

"Pete, you're looking rather agitated today," Sabina commented. "Is there something wrong?"

Truth was, I wasn't all right, not anymore. In fact, as soon as it was mentioned, I realised that I was actually far from all right. I walked over to where she was sitting, sat down across from her and almost immediately began laying off about some of my concerns.

"Listen, Sabina," I said, "this is all very well while I'm stuck here on Papa Stour, but what about when I leave? What happens then? You know, I don't feel like I've changed, not really, not where it probably matters most. I'm still me, at the end of the day!"

I could feel another of my impromptu rants threatening to emerge, and tried hard to contain my frustrations. Both Sabina and John could see my anguish and explained that it sometimes took a little while before things began to happen, and that I wasn't to worry too much.

"Not worry too much?" I retorted. "You have no idea what awaits me out there!"

I tried so hard to control myself, as tears began to form, but, of course, they didn't understand, and anyway, I didn't necessarily believe what they said, and so it flowed once more.

"Yeah, well, you tell me how come everybody in that Jackie Pullinger book gets completely set free? Go on, explain that to me!"

"Those are very different circumstances from what we have here, Pete," Sabina said.

"What? They need Christ more than I do? Is that what you're trying to tell me?"

I was levelling my questions at both of them, as I could see Sabina was unsettled by my outburst.

"Okay, tell me this, then. Why does everyone Jackie Pullinger come across end up being born again and speaking in tongues the minute she opens her mouth?"

Again silence, as I sat there waiting for an answer, my eyes flitting back and forth between them.

"What ...?" Sabina replied, with a nervous laugh. "Would you like to be able to speak in tongues or something?"

I wasn't sure if that was meant as some kind of joke, and found myself becoming really angry.

"No! No, of course I don't want to speak in bloody tongues!" I shouted. "I'm not some Chinese junkie! I just want to know, Sabina, that what I've done is real! If Jesus is real, and I have asked Him into my heart, why is nothing happening to me?"

Sabina looked at John, a knowing look passing between them as they somehow realised what was going on.

"Sounds like the devil talking, if you ask me, Sabina," John replied.

I didn't understand at the time what was meant by that comment, but I wasn't surprised to hear it – I mean, the devil was something I had believed in my whole life – but, boy, did it make me angry, so angry that, for once, I was completely silenced.

The three of us sat there looking at one another, not saying a word, until eventually they began to explain to me what was actually happening in *Chasing the Dragon*, and how it only really focused on the successes and not the failures, which I kind of understood.

Sensing what I was thinking – that I was a failure with no hope – they began telling me about their own experiences. Sabina, for instance, tried to explain how "things quite often happen very subtly over longer periods of time" while John was of the opinion that "God sometimes takes you by complete surprise, doing something totally unlike anything you've ever heard, or read about." They both agreed that it "wasn't always plain sailing, Peter" - not that I ever expected it to be.

I was thankful for their advice and largely accepted what they said, not necessarily because I understood it or for that matter, even believed them, but because I didn't want to further embarrass myself by arguing on. So, during the lull that followed they prayed for me, that God would reveal Himself to me in a powerful, life-changing way. And, shortly afterwards, all seemed well again.

Except, of course, it wasn't really. I just couldn't forget what John had said: "Sounds like the devil talking". That had really annoyed me; in fact, it had really hurt. But rather than retaliate, I decided to leave it at that and have an early night. I left Sabina and John, skipped supper, and instead went straight to my room.

* * *

I was sitting on a chair in front of the dresser unit, my feet up on the bed, reading the Bible. I had been power reading it since I gave my life to Jesus, hoping that it would somehow speak to me and give me some indication that what I had done was actually real.

I had just finished reading chapter 20 of John's Gospel, about Mary and the others finding the empty tomb and discovering that Jesus had been raised from the dead, and closing the Bible, I set it down on my dresser and sat there for what felt like ages, looking at myself in the mirror. I began thinking about the kind of person I had been throughout my life and the things I had done as a child. It all came flooding back to me: those feelings of hate I had harboured about myself; the things I had put my parents through; those thoughts of not wanting to live; the belief that I'd been a curse on my family.

A picture then burst into my mind of me sitting on the edge of my bed and shouting at my mother, "It's not *my* fault I'm the way I am! I never asked to be born!"

I had said some terrible things over the years to my parents, quite often blaming them for everything and wishing they'd never had me. But where did that coldness towards them, towards my life, come from? Why had I been so abusive? Why had I shunned them so? Why had I spent my whole life hurting them, when they had done nothing at all to deserve it?

I was thoroughly ashamed of the things I had done and felt this incredible sense of guilt welling up inside of me.

This is what your life has amounted to, Peter. You are a failure, a weak and pathetic, little failure. You have done nothing your whole life but hurt everyone who ever loved or cared about you, and now you have no one. You have been a complete fool in everything you've ever tried to do, and now look at you.

I found myself crying, watching in the mirror as tears ran down my face. I could taste their saltiness as they slipped inside the corners of my mouth, the flavour it seemed, of a broken life.

I then saw another picture in my mind and this time it was of my sister. She was waiting for me to arrive home, ready to receive me with so much hope in her heart, her face one big, happy smile. But something was telling me, as I walked towards her, that this very same bitter taste of tears was what awaited her, too.

The reality of my situation then hit home like never before, as I realised that the decision to change ultimately depended upon me, and it was for that reason alone that I anguished so. I knew only too well what I was like; good intentions always gave way to failure and the outcome was always one of self-destruction. I suddenly became extremely worried, not so much for me, but for her. How could I let that happen to her? How could I stop her from being hurt? How could I prevent it?

Suddenly it all became too much for me; the guilt and the sorrow were simply too much to bear – until I remembered something Andy had said: that if you give your heart to Christ, He will dwell within you, making you *more like Him.* And so I lifted my eyes up to the ceiling, and with my hands outstretched before me, I prayed.

"Dear God, I am so sorry. I am so, so sorry for the things that I have done. Please, will You forgive me and please, will You help me to change? I can't leave here and go back to being what I was before. If that happens I will lose the one and only person in this world who really cares about me, but I don't know if I have the strength to prevent it. Please, will You come and, please, will You help me now?"

I would be leaving the rehab in approximately three weeks' time, but I didn't feel that I had changed. I simply had no hope at all that life would ever be anything other than what it had been; life's experiences had taught me that. I hung my head in sheer despair.

"Please, please, please ....!" I sobbed and then, almost as a challenge, I cried out, "If you can raise Your Son, Jesus, from the dead then *please* help me now!"

As soon as I had finished saying those words, the tears stopped. I looked at myself a while longer in the mirror, trying to raise a little smile.

Well, at least you tried PJ, I thought, and then I went off to bed, where I quickly fell asleep. But it was a sleep that I will never forget, as I had a dream that was about to change my life.

* * *

I was in The Pond, playing pool with Biker Sean, when the door opened and in walked the "drummer" from the Manic Street Preachers. Amazed at who it was, although at the same time somehow aware that it looked nothing like him, I walked over to say "hello" and find out what he was doing there.

"Oh, I've just popped in on the off-chance to see if there was any pot on the go," he replied.

Surprised that anyone would come to The Pond for some cannabis resin, of all things – I mean, cocaine wouldn't have been a problem, and even crack or heroin, for that matter, was only ever a phone call away – but not wanting to disappoint, I asked around anyway.

"Look, I'm really sorry," I said, returning empty-handed, "there isn't any."

He smiled at me, as if he had been pulling my leg, and it was then that I somehow became aware that this wasn't just any old dream, there was something strangely real about this guy, something very familiar. And as I stood there looking at him, I seemed to be filled with this wonderful sense of peace.

"That's okay," he said, and then added, "actually the *real* reason I'm here, Peter, is to give you a lift."

Although that took me somewhat by surprise, I turned to where Biker Sean and his girlfriend, Sarah, were sitting. Sean looked up at me with a quizzical, almost suspicious look on his face, wondering what was going on. Without thinking, I simply smiled at them both, shrugged my shoulders and like an excited child waved them goodbye, as I turned and followed him out of the door.

Having left the bar together we climbed into his car, which was parked right outside the door, and then took off up this really steep hill, which, of course, doesn't exist outside The Pond.

The next thing I knew we were standing at the top of some steps, between two pillars, facing two enormous doors. I turned and looked at this man standing beside me, who simply smiled back.

I then became aware of something behind me, and so turned around to see what it was. What I then saw almost took my breath away. Stretching off into the horizon, under this amazing, golden sky, were all these pools of water that shimmered and danced as if made of pure crystal. It was one of the most beautiful things I had ever seen.

I was conscious of something happening, so I turned to face the doors again, just in time to see them opening. And to my surprise, who should be standing there but someone I took to be the lead singer of the "Manics", although, as was the case with the "drummer", I was aware that he looked nothing like him, while at the same time somehow looking very familiar. It was confusing, to say the least, but again, I just felt so at peace about the whole thing.

"Ah, Peter," he said, "I've been waiting for you. Come in and let me show you around."

I walked in through the door and found myself in the middle of what can only be described as a palace.

The "lead singer" asked how I was doing and I replied that I probably wasn't doing too well, at which he looked concerned. He then told me that they were going to record a new song and asked if I would like to hear it. Of course, I was hardly going to say "no", and nodded my head enthusiastically.

"That's great, and would you like to know what it's called?" he asked, and I nodded once more.

"It's called 'Send Away the Tigers'," he said, smiling at me.

I then followed them through a little doorway and into a room full of musical instruments. The "drummer" left us and positioned himself behind the drum kit. I then noticed there were three black Gospel singers, dressed in full choir attire, harmonising in one corner; there was a guitarist and a bass player, everything you would expect, I suppose.

He then told me to go and sit down while he sang this new song to me. Now, I can't remember the words, as I was so amazed that this should be happening, although I do remember they touched me very deep within, as did a lot of what the "Manics" sang about.

When it was over, he came and sat down next to me.

"So, Peter, what did you think of the song?"

"Yeah, it was all right," I replied, although it wasn't as good as the "Manics", which was the truth, and what's more he knew it, too, judging by the smile on his face. There was a brief moment of silence, until he spoke once more.

"Peter," he said, very softly, "tell me, what was your narrative name?"

Confused at this sudden change, I looked at him, trying to work out what he meant. My narrative name? What on earth did that mean? I also became very aware that this was of the utmost importance to me, and I so dearly wanted to understand. But try as I might I couldn't seem to grasp it, and I could feel myself becoming frustrated.

"What do you mean?" I pleaded with him. "What do you mean by my 'narrative name'?"

He could see the struggle in my eyes, as I tried desperately to comprehend what he was asking, but he just smiled and asked once more: "What ... was ... your narrative name?"

And then it hit me. I turned away from Him and hung my head in shame as I realised exactly Who was sitting next to me, and what He was asking of me. I had been right, this was no lead singer of the Manic Street Preachers, this was Jesus Christ, the Son of God, and He wanted me to open up my heart to Him, reveal to Him all those things buried deep within that made me who I was.

I sat there in silence, my head bowed, looking down at my feet, as my life flashed by before me. PJ, the liar, thief, usurper, failure, the breaker of hearts, destroyer of lives, alcoholic, drug addict, murderer ...

In what felt like a brief moment, I had seen myself for what I had always been, and it broke my heart. I had hurt so many people throughout my life, including myself. I had cursed my existence; I had cursed my parents; I had had the audacity to curse God for the various situations I found myself in throughout it. I had even made pacts with the devil, and all because I was angry at the world and hated who I was.

With so much anguish building up inside me, almost to the point of screaming for it to stop, I then saw all those things that had been done to me: the hurt I had felt; the sorrow and the shame of having been the cause of my father's ill health; that little boy who could never understand relationships; who had sought the love of his father and mother, but never felt he received any; the loneliness, the despair.

Yes, surely this was my narrative name, the story of who I was. I turned slowly to face Him, with the truth of who I was sticking hard in my throat, a part of me trying desperately to prevent it from being exposed, but with tears in my eyes, I whisperingly confessed, "I'm PJ."

I wouldn't have been surprised if He had turned away from me at that moment and left me there on my own, but He didn't. He reached out His hand and laid it upon my shoulder, looked at me, with these beautiful, big, blue eyes, and smiled at me in such a way that I knew instantly that He loved me. I knew that He always had, even through those times I had cursed His name, when I had wanted to die because of my hate for this life. All the while He had been there with me, sharing in my pain, holding me up and trying to reach me, every step of the way.

* * *

I burst awake from that dream and immediately on opening my eyes I knew that my life would never be the same again. I just lay there on my bed as tears began to run once more down my face, but these weren't tears of sorrow, they were tears of joy, of real joy – something I quickly realised I had never truly experienced before, and I was so very grateful for them, too.

Life could never be the same. Everything from that moment didn't only need to change, but demanded it. The very Creator of life itself had stepped down into my world, had taken the chains that held me and crushed them with His love.

CHAPTER 10

Leaving Papa Stour was relatively easy when the day finally came, although not for any reason other than I was desperate to find out who I was becoming.

Now, I suppose that might sound strange: "who I was becoming", but ever since that dream, or vision, or whatever it was, my whole way of thinking seemed to be changing. So much so, that I often wondered if it really was me this was happening to.

For nearly three whole weeks, I had wandered around North House in a sort of daze, with hopes and dreams of a "new me" and a "new life" jumping round in my head and heart. So, when the afternoon of Tuesday, 13 June, finally arrived, it was with great anticipation that I boarded the plane. And it certainly didn't disappoint.

Brian, who had been a wonderful support throughout, was waiting at Tingwall airstrip on the Shetland mainland to drive me to my sister's. He welcomed me back, made a comment about how much healthier I was looking and then, as we pulled out of the car park, he nodded towards a half-open packet of cigarettes.

"So, you'll want one of those, Peter?" he asked.

I looked at him then back at the cigarettes, but they just looked alien to me. Sticking my hand up my sleeve, I immediately peeled off one of those nicotine patches, opened up the window and threw it out, along with about half a dozen of those disgusting, half-chewed filters that had made their home in the bottom of my pockets.

"No, I don't think I will, Brian."

Where that came from was a bit of a mystery. I mean, it had never been my intention to stop smoking completely, hence the constant use of nicotine patches and plastic filters, but something clearly told me that I didn't need to smoke anymore. It really was peculiar.

And then, as we passed some of my old haunts like the Douglas Arms and the Thule Bar on our way through

Lerwick, the exact same thing happened. A thought from out of nowhere clearly told me that I wouldn't need to go there anymore either. This was even stranger, especially when I considered the significant role public bars had played in my life.

Within the space of little more than an hour, it had become plainly obvious that life did, indeed, promise to be very different. Gone was the old me and into Brian's car had stepped the new. But what would this person be like, and did he have the strength to live this out?

Those were hard questions, but they were also very real, considering what I used to be like. Yet as I pondered those thoughts throughout the remainder of that day, and especially during my prayer time at night, that same "Something" that had communicated with me in the car, began communicating with me again, and this time it was telling me to "trust in Him".

As concerned as I might be about what the future held, the minute that thought entered my mind I knew exactly what it meant, and it made so much sense. It wasn't a case of trusting in myself and whatever I could do, thank goodness, but of trusting in Him and what He had done.

I had left Papa Stour with a firm belief in Who this Jesus was and what's more, I trusted in all that the Gospels said about Him. It amazed me to think that this very same God, Jesus – the most significant man in all of history – was watching over me, promising to never leave me nor forsake me.

It was a truly wonderful revelation to have and as it turned out, an extremely timely one, too. Not only did it bring me great comfort at a time when I so desperately needed it, but it gave me a confidence that up until that night, at least, I had never before experienced in such a profound way. It truly was mind blowing.

Just how timely that revelation and boost to my confidence was became even more apparent in the days that followed.

WEDNESDAY 14 JUNE

I attended the Lerwick Health Centre for another liver function test. It was hoped that during the five or six weeks I hadn't been using drugs or alcohol my liver would show signs of improvement. It was an appointment I was very keen to attend, especially as everyone kept telling me how much healthier I was looking.

SUNDAY 18 JUNE

I had an appointment with a local Christian Fellowship (church) – an appointment, I have to admit, that I *wasn't* looking forward to! I had never walked in to a church all by myself before, but having become a Christian, a follower of the Lord Jesus Christ, I knew it was where I needed to be.

MONDAY 19 JUNE

I bumped into my old friend, Alastair Inkster, who having heard what was happening with me, recommended that I call about possible employment at a certain salmon factory. At the same time, Alastair also very kindly offered me a room in his new house, which I gladly accepted.

TUESDAY 20 JUNE

There I was at 7.15 a.m., standing in a changing room with 20 other people, donning waterproof overalls, rubber boots, rubber gloves and a Scottish Sea Farms hat.

Alastair's recommendation had proved fruitful, but it certainly wasn't where I had envisioned myself to be at that time of life: back living in Shetland and about to start work in a cold, wet, smelly, old salmon factory. However, as the day progressed, I had to concede that there were worse places I might have ended up – like dead.

I had another appointment with my doctor, this time for the results of the liver function test.

"Well, Peter," he said, "it isn't good news, I'm afraid. It turns out that your liver count has actually worsened."

Well, that didn't come as any great surprise really. I somehow knew that this was far from over, but what did surprise me was my attitude towards it.

"It's likely that we'll need to do more tests," he added, "but in the meantime, Peter, try not to worry about it."

"Absolutely fine," I replied, confidence oozing from every pore, "you just do whatever. I'll be okay."

No, I wasn't going to worry about it and what's more, I wasn't going to just ignore it either, like I would have done in the past; this time I was determined to see it through, whatever "it" turned out to be.

Enough had happened within such a short space of time to indicate that things were going to be interesting, and not only because of the choices that would undoubtedly be laid before me, but because of an amazing God, Who was willing and able to interact with me and Who, Biblical Scripture promised, had a plan and a purpose for the rest of my life.

With this in mind there really was little else for me to do but take Him at His word, simply "trust" and "obey", and see what happened.

* * *

Having moved in with Alastair to an attractive, little cottage in the picturesque village of Hamnavoe on the isle of Burra, approximately seven miles from my sister's, I was only ever in Lerwick at the weekends. It was certainly a lovely place to live, but as a consequence it meant I had considerably less time to spend with my family, something Vera voiced many concerns about. On a more positive note, it promised to make our weekends that little bit more special.

On Friday afternoons, after I finished work, I would take the work's bus into Lerwick with the aim of spending the weekend at my sister's. We would meet at my mother's apartment where we would order a Chinese takeaway, which our mother, even in her confusion, seemed to really enjoy. It was a great way to start the weekend and something we all looked forward to: Vera, me, and quite often one or both of my nieces.

It was during one such visit – perhaps only three weeks after coming out of rehab – that Vera finally broke the news that a move to a full-time dementia unit was imminent for Mum, and that we needed to make the most of our time with her. (It had been explained to Vera that once she was admitted, Mum wouldn't be able to leave, and worse still, it wouldn't be long before her mind went completely.)

The news didn't really come as a great shock to any of us – we all knew that this time would eventually arrive – but it was so very hard to believe that this was happening to her. She had always been so physically strong and healthy, in fact, she still was. It just didn't seem possible some days to believe that this woman, who had been so vibrant, would end her life in such an awful way.

Having experienced what I had, however, I wasn't quite willing to accept this, believing that God would somehow intervene. In my mind, there was something still to be done, and from what I had witnessed so far, surely God was the very One to do it. It was, I believed, a case of faithful prayer and great patience; a real test for any Christian.

Communing with God had taken priority in my life; in fact, one of the main reasons I had moved out to Burra was so I could spend more time with Him, through the reading of my Bible, and in prayer. Having a bedroom to myself instead of a sofa, and a housemate who worked away on the oilrigs instead of the constant hustle and bustle of my sister's, offered me plenty of opportunity to do exactly that.

Yes, I spent a lot of my time in Burra praying, and most of that praying for my mother. I would pray that she would be completely healed, restored to her former self, and as a result I would sometimes visualise myself walking into her apartment to find her sitting there on her sofa, completely free of Alzheimer's, saying something like: "Peter, what is going on? What are you doing here? Where's Vera? Where's Frankie? Why am I not at home in North Lochside?"

If anything, it was a wonderful daydream and one I would sometimes find myself thoroughly caught up in, quite often to the point where tears would fall. But *why*, why should it only be a daydream? Did God not hear me? Did He not care?

There was many a night when I poured out my heart to God about my mother, but it didn't seem to matter how hard I prayed or objected to His ways, nothing I said or did ever made much difference. Of course, the longer it went on without any sign of improvement, the more obvious it became that Vera was probably right, and that realistically the only thing we could do was enjoy whatever time we had left.

And so, even with all the prayer and patience in the world, in the back of my mind I knew that was what we all needed to do, and, thankfully, that's what we did.

On Friday evenings, we would meet at King Erik House and enjoy a takeaway together. On Saturdays we would meet our mother and other family members at the British Legion Social Club, where they often took her for a bar lunch. Then, later in the afternoon, Vera and I would call along her apartment and sit for a couple of hours chatting with her while watching early evening telly. On Sunday mornings, Vera would collect my mother and take her to her flat where, after I returned from the morning service at the church I was attending, we would all enjoy a dinner together.

As a family we really tried to cram in as much as we could at the weekends, but Sunday dinner, for me, was that little bit more special. It brought with it many a happy memory of Sunday afternoons at North Lochside, something we all enjoyed while growing up, although, as my sister joked, "In those days we didn't all have to wait until you came home from church before we could eat!"

Yes, a lot had changed since then and I did, indeed, go to church, but although church was something I had been really excited about, it wasn't really what I had hoped.

* * *

After attending that first morning service on June 18, the fact that I went back the following week was a miracle in itself; it simply hadn't been a good experience for me. But I returned the following week, nonetheless, hoping it would be a little better, only to find that it wasn't. In fact, each week would always be worse than the one before it.

So, what was wrong? What could cause such a feeling within a church? Well, it wasn't the fault of any individual or group, or anything of that nature, which could easily have been resolved; no, it was something entirely different and certainly not what I expected to experience in the house of God.

When I attended that first service – having walked back and forth past the door about half a dozen times before finally plucking up enough courage to enter – I had made for a seat at the back. I didn't want to have to talk with anyone, or make eye contact even, preferring instead to keep to myself as much as I possibly could.

As soon as the worship began, I stood up along with everyone else. I even joined in a little, too, although singing very quietly. I listened as the church notices were read out, and partook of the bread and wine during Communion. I watched, with great amusement, a five-minute children's slot, and even put a few quid in the basket when it was time for the offering.

Up until that point, everything seemed fine. In fact, I would go as far as to say I was actually enjoying myself. It was only when the pastor began to share the Word of God that I realised something wasn't quite right.

Almost from the moment he started preaching, I began to hear voices in my head – not so much audible voices, perhaps, but very strong thoughts similar to those I had already been experiencing – except these were of a very different nature; these were extremely negative.

What are you doing?

You don't belong with these people.

Look at them, PJ! They don't even want you here!

I remember looking up at one point towards a section of the church, just to see what everyone else was doing, and catching a few people looking at me.

See ... They don't really want the likes of you here.

You are never going to fit in.

They don't even like you, PJ.

And all through the sermon it never once let up. In fact, the more the pastor preached, the more intense it became. All I seemed able to do, in my defence, was shut my eyes and pray, hoping that this would somehow block it out. Well, it was either that or I would have to leave.

Yet I somehow knew, even then, that if I walked out of the meeting half way through it, I would never go back. So, I just dug my heels in and struggled on throughout the remainder of the service as best I could, but the minute it was over I bolted out of the door.

I remember walking home from that first meeting feeling sorely dejected. I mean, what was I supposed to make of that experience? I had been so looking forward to it, and it had turned into a complete nightmare.

God, however, Who I had been calling out to all through it, had the answer ...

By the time I arrived back at my sister's, my mother, who had been there for an hour, was pacing around the living room looking confused and a little frightened, as was often the case.

I said "hello" and managed to get her to sit down with me on the sofa. I then began to tell her about church; about all the people singing; the musicians playing in the corner; the big wooden cross on the platform; the children's slot; the breaking of bread; the preacher with his Bible in his hand – and it suddenly dawned on me how much of it I had taken in, and how much of it I had actually enjoyed.

Now, this came as a bit of a surprise to me. Here I was, speaking about church with so much joy and genuine excitement – even getting a little carried away at times – and in turn it was affecting my mother in a positive way! It was quite amazing, considering her short attention span.

Vera, standing by watching us, and equally amazed at my mother's response, was also interested to hear about my church experience.

"So, Peter, does this mean that you'll be going back next week?" she said, laughing a little. (I think she had been surprised that morning to discover that I had gone to church.)

"Oh, yeah, without a doubt, Sis!" I replied.

The truth is, as difficult as it had been, I *did* want to go back and what's more, I went back the following week, and the week after that, and the week after that. This was in spite of the fact that those voices kept on goading me, never once decreasing, only ever becoming worse – yet I kept going back for more. But why did I keep putting myself through all that?

Well, that's easy. You see, every time I returned home to my sister's and sat down next to my mum and told her all about church, I felt something very beautiful stirring in my heart, which not only had a wonderful effect on me, but had a wonderful effect on my mother, too. She would sit there listening to my story – very quiet, very still – with a lovely, little smile that couldn't help but light up the faces of everyone in that room.

So, although I struggled desperately through each church meeting, I was absolutely determined to keep going. As difficult and as hurtful as it was, voices or no voices, I went just so that I could sit with my mother on a Sunday afternoon and catch, with every word, a tiny glimpse in those lovely smiling eyes of the mother I longed to be with again.

Yes, God, in His infinite wisdom, was able to take what could so easily have been a negative, faith-destroying experience and turn it into something beautiful instead.

* * *

Spiritually, life at that time was very interesting, as you can probably imagine. The only good thing to come out of it, it seemed, was my mother's response, and I was willing to tolerate it for her sake, but physically, things for me were about to take a turn for the worse.

At roughly 5 p.m. on Friday, 30 June, I had not long left my mother's apartment and was walking along the road to the Red Dragon Takeaway, via the convenience store where I was to pick up a *Shetland Times*, when my mobile phone rang. I pulled it out of my pocket, thinking it would be my sister, but instead I saw a number that I didn't recognise.

My first reaction was not to answer it. Well, it could have been anyone: Itchy, Scratchy, or worse still, their odd job man, Johnny the Hunchback. After six weeks of no contact I wasn't in the humour to listen to some overly-excited Scouser describe in great detail what would happen to me, and more than likely my family, too, if I didn't return to Aberdeen with their supposed £7,000.

I let it ring off and then stuck it back in my pocket, but almost immediately I regretted it.

Why worry about it, Peter? What can they possibly do to you, especially now that you have God on your side?

And, then, as if to test my faith, it rang once more.

I reluctantly pulled the phone from my pocket and this time I answered it.

"Is that Peter Jamieson?" the strange voice asked. "It is Dr Jackson here – from the Lerwick Health Centre."

A little relieved, I stopped in my tracks, not wanting to walk into a shop in mid-conversation, and out of habit started doing that stupid little phone thing of pacing back and forth and round in circles.

"Look, Peter, I have the results of that test. Where are you right now? Is it okay for me to tell you over the phone?"

"Yeah, fire away," I replied.

Well, if he was prepared to tell me over the phone, it had to be good news, right?

"The results show that you are negative for HIV, but I'm afraid you're positive for hepatitis C."

And just like that, I had the results.

"Are you all right, Peter? Would you like to come and see me?" he quickly asked.

"Yeah ... No, I'm fine, thanks, all the same," I replied. "I'm collecting a takeaway for me mam anyway."

I stopped in my tracks and lifted my face heavenwards.

"So, what happens now, then?"

"Well, come in and see me next week and we'll discuss it, but in the meantime ..."

Funnily enough, I knew what it was he was about to say, and, no, I wasn't going to worry about it.

* * *

By the end of July I had moved out of Alastair's and was renting a room from a work colleague named Davy, who had a house in the village of Scalloway, about three miles away. A problem had arisen concerning my lift to work in the mornings, forcing me into the move, but having said that, it felt somehow very right.

Living in Burra had been a wonderful start, giving me the confidence to face certain issues – like being in an environment where alcohol was consumed – as well as spending long periods of time on my own. I fully appreciated Alastair's generosity, which at times went far and above the call of duty, but Scalloway had certain advantages that Burra very clearly lacked.

There were more shops to choose from, the bus to and from Lerwick was more frequent, even running later at night, and the company I worked for would be relocating there in a matter of months, which meant an end to a 40-mile round trip to and from work every day. Scalloway also happened to be home to my Aunt Margaret, who I hadn't clapped eyes on since my father's funeral, but most important of all, I fully believed in my heart it was where God wanted me to be, and this was the ultimate reason for the move.

Now, there are many reasons why I might have come to that conclusion, but let's just say the events that followed are in themselves sufficient.

Having reacquainted myself once more with Aunt Margaret, I quickly settled into life in Scalloway. Getting to and from work each day was somewhat easier, as the work's bus passed through the village, and my aunt, who I would always visit after I finished my shift, made me so very welcome. She was extremely kind towards me, although well aware of the lifestyle I had led – and just as aware of the reasons I had returned to Shetland – but she hadn't been fazed by any of it. She welcomed me into her home with no reservations, and even after listening to my story she never once judged me or questioned why I chose to do the things I did. Instead, she simply promised to be there for me if I ever needed her.

Yes, Aunt Margaret became a wonderful source of encouragement; someone I knew I could confide in and as unexpected as that all was, she became a very dear friend.

Not long after I arrived on the scene, my aunt was to have another rather strange visitor turn up on her doorstep: a man by the name of Sverrir Halldórsson. Because Margaret's home doubled as a B & B, she was quite used to people arriving out of the blue, but his arrival was something a little different.

Sverrir was from Iceland and he was in the publishing business. He had come to Shetland to oversee the compilation of a book, but he seemed to have no way of knowing how long it would take and, therefore, had no idea how long he would need the room for.

“Two months, three months, perhaps six months, a whole year even!” he had joked, but the truth was, he really had no clue – something Margaret found a little odd.

Later on the afternoon of his arrival, my aunt explained to me – in great detail – how this rather dapper young man had seemingly tried every B & B from Lerwick to Scalloway, and the only one with a room available had been hers. She then went on to describe his mannerisms, the clothes he wore, how little luggage he had, his constant comings and goings, and the calls and messages galore to his mobile phone. I must admit to being very impressed with her observational skills, but she had found it all a bit peculiar and felt it necessary to be a little cautious.

A day or two later, however, Aunt Margaret’s tone had changed and she had greatly warmed to her new guest. She also informed me that they had spent a lot of time talking and she had told him a little about me: how I had just moved to Scalloway; that I was working in a salmon factory; that she had taken me under her wing, and especially that I had been spending the last few nights fishing for mackerel from the shore.

Not entirely sure where this conversation was going, she then dropped it on me that Sverrir had requested joining me on one of my trips, a request which she took upon herself to grant.

I must admit that came as something of a shock. I mean, I was glad she finally felt more comfortable with this man, and didn’t really mind that she wanted me to take him out; after all, I had been fishing for mackerel the previous three or four nights (and was always quick to brag about how many I had caught the day after).

But what could I possibly offer this man from Iceland, other than a lesson in how to fish? That was my main worry. I was useless when it came to making conversation. Even those who knew me well had a hard enough job, so how on earth was I going to manage with a foreigner?

Of course, I didn't want to let Margaret down; after all, she was being incredibly good to me. So, that evening I called along with a spare fishing rod for her new guest.

It was very strange, but Sverrir and I seemed to hit it off from the outset. I walked into the kitchen as he sat at the table finishing his evening meal and we were able to converse without any problem.

It would be true to say that I had never felt more at peace with a stranger than I did at that first meeting with Sverrir. There was something about him that immediately alleviated all nervousness, or perhaps I was simply becoming more confident.

As promised, I took him sea fishing from the rocky ledges just along the shore from the B & B. Sensing there was a bit of fun to be had, my aunt even pulled on a pair of rubber boots, deciding she wasn't going to miss out, and a great time was had by all. We chatted and laughed as we fished from the shore, Aunt Margaret even helping with the fish we caught. It was a great time together, which carried on back at her house as she fried up a late supper of freshly-caught mackerel – mostly caught by me, of course!

Feeling very relaxed with Sverrir and thoroughly enjoying his company, I then braved telling him a little of my story, and the reason why I was back in Shetland. It was then I discovered why I had felt so at ease with him; Sverrir was a born-again Christian.

After listening to me for a while, he told us about himself and the book he was putting together. It was to be part of a set of books connecting the Old Norse islands: Iceland, Greenland, Faroe Islands and the Shetland Islands. A percentage of the proceeds would go to help fund various Christian organisations, like an orphanage in Africa. He then brought out a portfolio with photographs and letters from various high-ranking officials substantiating his claims. It really was most impressive.

Having become good friends, I would meet with Sverrir every afternoon when I finished work, or perhaps later on in the evenings if he was off somewhere on business. I would also go with him around the island as he set about putting this book together. He would quite often invite me to some of the meetings he had with the various local dignitaries who were contributing written articles for the book – each author depicting a different aspect of life in Shetland – always introducing me as his "local advisor". I just had to hope that whoever we were going to visit didn't know me from my past – something Sverrir said I no longer needed to be worried about, as I was a changed man.

Yes, it was all very interesting, a good laugh and a time of much learning, although perhaps not for the above reasons. You see, Sverrir had marvellous faith, as well as an impressive knowledge of the Bible, which he would readily expound as we travelled all over the face of Shetland in his rented car; some days all he would ever talk about was Jesus.

It was remarkable that I should have met in with such a man, and again it left me wondering. *Has God, in His infinite wisdom, now sent me Sverrir?* As peculiar as my aunt perhaps found him, I couldn't help but think so.

* * *

It was a Saturday afternoon – August 5, the day after my 39th birthday – and to celebrate I had been taken to an agricultural show in a little village called Voe, about 20 miles north of Lerwick. By this time I had been running around with Sverrir for a little over a week, and although this was meant as a treat for me – agricultural shows not something I would normally have chosen to attend – I knew it was really for him, and his insatiable appetite for meeting local people.

Arriving at the show, Sverrir parked the car and before I knew what was going on, he sprung open his door and went running off across the car park in the direction of this big, blue, double-decker bus. Emblazoned along its side, in massive letters, were the words: "Live Life to the Full – Follow Jesus."

I just shook my head and followed on after him at a more relaxed pace, knowing how impetuous he could be. By the time I caught up with him, he was doing what he did best – speaking with the driver of this rather elaborate vehicle.

"Peter, this is my friend, Brother Clifford!"

Sverrir had recently spent some time in the Faroe Islands, where only weeks before he had, on a number of occasions, bumped into Brother Clifford and his "Jesus Bus". I had never in my life seen such a thing as the "Jesus Bus", and as for Brother Clifford, well, he seemed a bit of an enigma, too. He was a funny, little man, perhaps in his late fifties, very upright in stature, his head held high. He had wavy, grey hair, which looked like it could do with a good comb, and the sharpest set of blue eyes I'd ever seen.

"I'm very pleased to meet you, Peter. Now, are you a Christian?" he asked.

Brother Clifford, I quickly noticed, was somewhat direct. I nodded my head.

"Ah, that's great, but are you a born-again believer?" he enquired, those piercing blue eyes of his locked firmly onto mine.

"Eh ... I ... Eh ..."

"Tell me, Peter, have you died to the things of this world and do you now live for Christ Jesus?" he asked, firmly.

"Eh, yes! Yes, I have!" I replied.

"Great, then you must be. Now, come aboard my bus, drink coffee with me, and tell me all about you," he said, releasing my hand.

Having shown me around the bus and listened to Sverrir's news, Brother Clifford then turned his attention to me, inviting me to share my testimony with him. We sat together drinking coffee as I nervously told him my story, and when I had finished he looked at me thoughtfully, reached out his hand and began to pray.

"Father," he began, "we thank You for all that You have done in this young man's life. Please grant my brother the strength to do that which You have called him to do, give him boldness when testifying of Your mercy and grace, but most of all, grant him Your peace, that wonderful, wonderful peace, the peace that transcends all understanding, that he may hear Your voice above everything else."

I remember thinking it rather strange that he should mention voices, but I didn't read too much into it then.

* * *

Life with Sverrir was non-stop. He was on the go wherever we went, always stopping to speak with everyone he met, given even the slightest opportunity, and quite often making them himself.

It didn't surprise me that he should already be acquainted with Brother Clifford, albeit from a few chance meetings a couple of weeks before in the Faroe Islands. Coincidences of this nature, I was sure, were rife in Sverrir's world. But I couldn't help thinking there was more to all this than met the eye; it was all just a little, well, a little weird.

We left Brother Clifford's bus and wandered around the show, me thinking that things couldn't get any more bizarre, and then I spotted him ... This time it was someone *I* knew, someone perhaps on par with Brother Clifford, but very possibly even more of an enigma: a man by the name of Andrew Harmsworth.

Andrew was one of the many people at my church who I tried hard to avoid. He was just too loud for me – too friendly, even – which made me somewhat uneasy. He was quite a big man, probably in his early sixties, who always seemed so full of joy and energy. You would often see him dancing around like a Native American during Sunday morning worship, or rushing around at the end of the service with a piece of paper in his hand, trying to raise awareness of some new government policy that had a chance of affecting our right to be "Christians in our own country", or something along those lines.

Without ever having spoken to Andrew, I always made a point of avoiding him, and I would have given him a wide berth again that day – except Sverrir was already onto him.

"Ah, Sverrir, did you say? How lovely it is to meet you!" I heard him bellow, as they stood together shaking hands.

I followed up behind them and drew up a seat, seeing as how we were now in the midst of a Christian beverage tent, of all things.

"And so you two know each other?" I heard him ask.

"Yes, this is my friend, Peter," Sverrir replied.

"Oh, you don't have to tell me who this is. I know this chap, all right," he said, grabbing hold of my hand and shaking it vigorously. "Yes, you are Peter Jamieson. You've been coming to our fellowship for the last month or so, and every time I come looking for you at the end of the meeting, you are nowhere to be seen!" He laughed. "You must scarper out of the door faster than a scalded cat, eh?"

There was certainly no denying that I was, indeed, that man, the one who bolted for the door at the end of every service, and strangely, I suddenly felt a little convicted about it, and even more so of the feelings that I'd had about him. For, as we talked, I quickly realised that Andrew was a very gentle, kind man – and nothing at all like I'd painted him – at least not outside of church, anyway!

Then, just when I thought nothing untoward was going to happen and he was, in fact, quite normal, he suddenly sprung it on me.

"So, Peter, seeing as you're celebrating your birthday, what better way to end it than at a prayer meeting tonight at the Salvation Army hall?"

Sverrir's ears pricked up right away.

"Prayer meeting? Why, yes, that would be most excellent. What time must we be there and where is this place?"

That had made Sverrir's day, I could just tell, and recent experience told me there would be no getting out of it. What's more, something from that time of prayer with Brother Clifford told me it was the right thing to do. I needed to start facing up to things; I needed to be bolder, and stop running away.

I considered it briefly. “Yeah,” I replied, thoughtfully, “okay then.”

By the time we arrived at the Salvation Army hall, all the seats had been taken, with everyone sitting in a big circle. Andrew, just as I expected, was exuberant in his welcome.

“Ah, how wonderful! Bring out some chairs for our very special guests, Peter and Sver-ree-er.” (He had a funny way of pronouncing the name, which he never quite managed to get right in all the time Sverrir was in Shetland.)

To say that I suddenly didn’t want to be there would be an understatement. I could have happily turned round and walked out, but everyone just looked so pleased to see us. Chairs suddenly appeared beneath us, just as Andrew asked if we would share a little about ourselves.

For Sverrir, this was like having all his birthdays come at once and he talked for at least five minutes. I, on the other hand, was extremely brief, sharing only my name and how long I had been a Christian.

Andrew thanked us for our contribution then explained who they (SIT) were.

“We are the Shetland Intercessors Team, a prayer group. Basically, we’re a bunch of Christians who meet once a month to pray specifically for the needs of Shetland, and especially for those in authority.”

I could tell it was something he took very seriously.

I looked around the room and noticed one or two familiar faces from the fellowship I attended, as well as Brother Clifford who having met my eyes gave me a reassuring nod. I sat very still after that, my eyes fixed firmly on the floor, for fear of someone speaking to me, and I tried to focus instead on what was being said.

Andrew began by reminding everyone of the last meeting, what they had been praying about, any prophetic words that had been given, and then he asked if anyone knew of any answers to prayer. A few people offered updates on various issues; for instance, there were interesting developments surrounding the fishing grounds off Shetland, with an increase in white fish catches reported in a national newspaper, as well as one or two issues concerning the local council.

After a little more discussion, Andrew proposed that they all begin their time of intercession (praying for other people). I immediately closed my eyes, relieved that not only would everyone else have their eyes closed, too, but I could begin to pray against the voices that had begun, not just as I sat down, or when Andrew started speaking, but the moment we entered the building.

PJ, what do you think you are doing here?

You don't belong.

These people don't want the likes of you, remember.

You're just going to make a fool of yourself, and they'll all see you for what you really are.

And so on.

With my head bowed and my eyes firmly closed, I did all I knew to do and prayed like never before.

Please, God, why does this always happen to me? What is wrong with me? Please, please, take this away from me!

Tears began to well up in my eyes; I was just so heartbroken and utterly sick of it. For six or seven weeks, this was what I'd had to endure, week in and week out at church, and it was driving me mad.

I must have been praying for at least half an hour, my heart heavier than I had ever felt it before, when with one final effort – before standing up and walking out of the room and very possibly away from Christianity for good – I cried out from the very depths of my being.

Dear Lord God, if this is really *where I belong, then please,* please, *will you take this away from me? Please show me a sign that this is real, that this is worth all the pain, because I can't go on like this any longer; it's too much for me to bear.*

With those words said, I suddenly felt a gentle, warm glow flowing through my body. A little startled, I opened my eyes to see what was going on, but everyone else seemed to be carrying on as normal, their heads bowed or tilted back facing the ceiling, with their hands held high in the air. I then bowed my head once more, and as I was about to close my eyes, I noticed something very peculiar. Just above my hand, at the top of my left wrist, something had visibly changed. I pulled up my sleeve to have a proper look and my heart started to race.

Two small lumps, caused by careless injecting, had completely vanished. I started to shake and quickly pulled back the sleeves on both arms, looking from one to the other, back and forth. I couldn't believe what I was seeing! My arms had been completely cleaned!

I lifted my head and looked around the room at everyone peacefully praying.

"Eh ... Excuse me ... Please!" I announced, boldly.

Everyone stopped what they were doing and looked at me, puzzled, until I began to explain to them who I was, how I had come to faith in Christ, how I came to be there that night, and what had just taken place.

The whole room erupted in a chorus of Hallelujahs and Praise the Lords, as well as one or two holy expressions I had never heard before. We had a truly fantastic evening after that – of praise, worship and prayer aplenty – and I thoroughly enjoyed every minute of it!

Needless to say, church the following morning was very different. Completely gone were those feelings of shame and worthlessness, and silenced at long last were those voices.

Yes, all through that Sunday morning meeting I felt peace like never before. It was as if a warm blanket had been wrapped round me, an impenetrable, indestructible blanket that somehow protected me from those outside forces that had been trying so hard to drive me out. It was, I knew, the peace that Brother Clifford had prayed about, the "peace of God that transcends all understanding".

So utterly thankful was I for that peace that I stood up at the end of the meeting and asked if I could speak. After a bemused look from Pastor Jamie, unsure, perhaps, of what I wanted to say, there I was, a few seconds later, standing behind the pulpit, once again telling my story. And just like the night before, the place erupted with the sound of clapping and God's people praising His name.

Back at my sister's, I didn't say anything to begin with about what had happened at the Salvation Army hall, for fear of what she might think. It was, however, noticed how different I looked as soon as I walked in the door. Of course, I was sorely tempted to tell them all, but chose instead to see to my mother, who was pacing around the floor looking very confused.

Taking her by the hand, I set her down on the sofa and, full of the Holy Spirit, began telling her all about church, about how fantastic it was. And yet again, she sat there as quiet as a mouse, smiling at me until I finished my story. But this time, when I finished, something happened that took us all by complete surprise.

My mother spoke out.

"I would like to go to church with you sometime."

There was a silence in the room. Vera, who was sitting directly across from us, looked utterly shocked. For the first time in absolutely ages, our mother had strung together a meaningful sentence.

We looked at one another, my sister shaking her head, but I wasn't about to let this slip. I turned back to my mother.

"Are you sure? Because if you really want to go, I'll take you."

I glanced at Vera.

"Peter, you know fine well what she's like – or maybe you don't! You have no idea what she might do!" she warned.

I was shaking, full of excitement. I didn't know what to do, and then suddenly I did. *If she says it again I will take her, no matter what,* I thought.

I turned to my mother a second time.

"Mam, what did you just say to me?"

And without hesitation, she replied, "I want to go to church with you."

That was it. I had made up my mind. The following Sunday I would attempt to take her with me to church.

Later that day, after we walked our mother home, I could tell that Vera wasn't at all comfortable with what I was planning to do, and so I decided to tell her about the miracle of the night before. I thought it might just give her the assurance she needed.

As we walked along the road, just the two of us, I explained to her about the Voe Show and the people I met there: Brother Clifford and his "Jesus Bus", Andrew Harmsworth at the Christian coffee tent, and then the Shetland Intercessors Team at the Salvation Army. It must have all sounded utterly alien to her. I then told her what had happened while I was there.

I really didn't know what she was going to think of this story. I mean, without proof it might seem a little far-fetched. But, unknown to me I had shown her my wrists and arms that very first night I arrived at her flat. Vera tried to remind me of the conversation we'd had at the time, and how it had led to me showing her my wrists, but I had no recollection of it.

We stopped in the middle of the high street as she asked me to pull back my sleeves. Immediately her eyes widened, her mouth fell open and I saw Vera completely silenced, which is not something that happens very often.

* * *

By the time I arrived at King Erik House the following week, helped by a member of staff my mother was all ready to go. I said "hello", told her who I was and where I was taking her, and without saying a word, she reached out and took a hold of my hand.

We then began the walk along the Hillhead, just the two of us, on a beautiful, sunny morning, and when we were almost half way there, I felt a sudden urge to ask her something. We stopped walking and I turned to her.

"Mam, I'm taking you to my church today and, well, I go there every week to worship Jesus."

She looked at me, not saying anything.

"Mam, Jesus is real. He helped me. He came to me and He changed my life."

Still she said nothing. I knew this was probably going nowhere, but I felt the need to carry on.

"Mam, do you know Jesus?"

I didn't really expect a reply and I almost resumed walking, thinking this a waste of time and beginning to feel a little foolish, perhaps, but I was in for a surprise.

"Yes," she asserted, looking right into my eyes. "Yes, I know Jesus. Maggie used to take me and the boys to Sunday school whenever it was on. Yes, I know Jesus!" And she smiled at me, that very same smile I longed for each week. (Maggie was an old lady who used to live with my grandparents and help look after their eight children.)

That was all I had wanted to hear, and I wanted Him to hear it, too.

You heard her, God. You heard what she said. My mother knows You; she knows You and, therefore, she belongs to You. As Your word says, nothing can take us from Your hand.

I was just stunned – amazed. I could hardly move from the spot, I'd had such a shock. I put my arms around her and under a beautiful, blue sky, as the sun shone upon us, I held her tight.

"Thank you, God," I whispered.

What a wonderful surprise that had been that morning, and what a feeling it then was to be standing next to my mother in a church, holding her hand and singing the praises of God.

A little before the service ended we had to leave, as she was becoming increasingly agitated. Once outside she seemed to lose all recollection of where she had been and what she had been doing there. I tried to jog her memory as we walked back to her apartment, so that at least something of our morning might stay with her, if only for a little while, but no matter how hard I tried, she became more and more confused, until I gave up on it for fear of upsetting her.

Of course, it was sad, but in the great scheme of things I knew it didn't really matter. To me, the whole exercise had been completely worthwhile. I had managed to take my mother to church like I had promised, and I had heard her confess to knowing Christ, which had been my most fervent prayer. I had even heard her singing His praises while standing next to her in church – something I never, ever thought I would see happen. So, yes, the whole exercise from beginning to end, as far as I was concerned, exceeded all of my expectations.

It had been a very special time and I truly thanked God for it. This, I believe, was a gift from Him and the answer to so many tearful prayers.

Mum's health declined rapidly, and so it was the first and last time I was able to take her to church. Within four weeks she was admitted to Viewforth House.

CHAPTER 11

I think it's safe to say that until I became a Christian baptism wasn't particularly high on my all-time list of "things to do before I die". In fact, baptism wasn't something I had considered before in any context whatsoever. But, on Saturday morning, September 2, 2006, that changed. On a beach directly below North House, in the freezing cold waters of Papa Stour – and also in the path of an on-coming northerly wind – witnessed by friends and family, as well as a scattering of islanders looking on from afar, I underwent what is called a full immersion baptism.

It was, without a doubt, one of the most important days of my life, and certainly one that I will never forget.

Standing with nervous anticipation, waist deep in the Atlantic Ocean, with Pastor Jamie on one side and John Jarrett on the other, I faced shoreward to where a group of people stood watching me. They were my sister, Vera, my Aunt Margaret, my cousin, Lynne, and her two daughters, Sverrir, Aaron, Becki, Andy and Sabina, Bertie and Rhona, Scott and Catherine.

With my arms crossed over my chest, I pulled them ever tighter as the verses being spoken over me neared completion.

"In the name of the Father, and of the Son, and of the Holy Spirit ..."

Deep breath ...

In that brief moment before going under, I stood amazed at how far I had actually come, and just as incredible was the realisation of how much of myself I was prepared to give. But then again, I had surely witnessed enough of God's amazing grace by that point to know that living for me – or for anything other than Christ Jesus – was worthless, a waste of precious time.

Beneath the water they lowered me – my life at that point still very much my own – then, having proclaimed to

God only a few seconds before that I would "die to myself and all this world has to offer", as well as boldly renouncing "the devil and all the ways of evil", I was raised from beneath the waves into what the Bible describes as "new life".

Yes, baptism, by my reckoning, was extremely significant. Not only did it mark an important milestone in my development as a Christian, but having made such a personal, and at the same time very public, declaration of faith, it seemed to open up a doorway into a whole new level of spirituality.

About an hour after coming up from the water, as everyone sat together enjoying a buffet, I became very aware that something tremendously powerful had taken place; I clearly wasn't the same person who had gone under the water.

I remember thinking long and hard all afternoon about what it could be, but I couldn't quite put my finger on it. It was a strange feeling, that much was obvious, but it was also a very good feeling, too. It was as if I had gained a heightened sense of confidence – an absolute assurance, perhaps – of having received something very precious. What that was, however, I had no idea, and what it meant to me, I understood even less.

Later that night, as Sverrir and I drove back to Scalloway, just the two of us, I tried to explain to him what had happened after the baptism and the conclusion I had come to, hoping he would shed some light on the matter.

"It's as if I have been given some kind of authority, although it's somehow more than that. It's not just any authority, Sverrir, it's *His* authority," I said. "Does that make any sense to you?"

Sverrir glanced quickly round, looked me straight in the eyes and then, turning his attention back to the winding, single-track road of West Burrafirth, he answered in all seriousness.

"Peter, that is exactly it! You have, indeed, been given authority and, yes, it is His authority." Sensing my confusion, he went on. “Look, don’t worry about what that means, I’m pretty sure you will find out soon enough.”

I think it was at that moment I finally realised that there could be no going back for me. No matter how much it may have been lurking in my subconscious – that if none of this worked out I could always revert, at least to some degree, back into my old life – I knew from that moment on I no longer had that luxury.

And to be perfectly honest, it was a little unnerving.

* * *

Within the space of a couple of months, there followed a few changes to my personal circumstances, all of which added rather significantly to the quality of my life. For instance, I moved from my lodgings into a house on Scalloway’s Main Street, which belonged to Andy and Sabina. Almost overnight I went from renting a small, single bedroom to living in a four-bedroomed house, which I pretty much had all to myself – unless my landlords decided to come out of Papa Stour for the weekend. Also, the company I was employed with had moved to new premises on the Scalloway Pier and so, instead of a 40-mile round trip to and from work every day, I had a ten-minute walk, there and back. But it was everything I suddenly found myself involved in that really had a profound effect on me.

Without particularly realising it, I had become quite a regular at the Scalloway Methodist Church Sunday evening services, which meant I was attending two services on a Sunday: one in Lerwick in the morning and one in Scalloway in the evening. I had also become a regular at the all-important church Home Group, which was held on Tuesday nights at Bertie and Rhona’s house, and I’d been going along to a Bible study, which was held at the Scalloway Methodists on Thursday evenings. In addition to all that, I had offered my services musically and joined the church worship group, which met on Friday nights.

Yes, as far as following Christ went, I had quickly become a very busy boy, indeed, involving myself in just about everything I possibly could. In fact, four nights out of seven, I was completely committed to either one thing or another to do with the church. Yet there was never any question in my mind about whether I was doing the right thing or not. I somehow knew that it was doing me an amazing good, especially being surrounded by so many people who knew and understood the needs of a young Christian like me.

With all that was going on, and with so many people watching out for me, I honestly didn't think that anything could stand in my way. I had never felt happier, never felt so safe, and never felt so good about myself. I was even highly optimistic about the future. This was in complete contrast to how I had felt prior to asking Jesus into my life.

Even the concerns I may have had about my health didn't appear to bother me as much, especially concerning the hep C, which to my knowledge was still affecting my liver. I just felt so at peace with myself and the world around me, calm like never before.

* * *

Now, there were two very important events that I believe deserve credit for putting me into such a good place. The first was undoubtedly the baptism on Papa Stour, which had somehow filled me with this supernatural sense of "authority", and the second, which I hadn't expected to affect me nearly as much as it did, was giving my full testimony (telling the story of how I came to faith in Christ) for the first time.

Shortly after attending the Scalloway Methodist church, I had been approached by this rather wonderful gentleman, the Reverend Malcolm McCall. Having heard a little of my story at one of his Bible studies, he had asked if I would accompany him to what he called a "Sankey Night" – a monthly meeting held at a little Methodist chapel in a village called Girlsta where, amongst other things, they sing from the Sankey hymn book – and there share my full testimony.

Up until then I had only ever shared very briefly about what had happened to me: once with Brother Clifford, once at the Salvation Army, once at the church I attended in Lerwick, once at Home Group, and once at Malcolm's Bible study. However, I had never intentionally addressed a whole congregation and to be honest, I wasn't particularly keen on speaking publicly about what had happened, especially when I had no idea who would be there.

The temptation, as always, was to shy away from it, but instead I found myself agreeing, after it was explained to me how important it was to testify (tell our story) for the benefit of others.

A week or so later I was picked up from my house and taken to Girlsta Chapel where after a few good-going hymns I was invited to the front of the church to share my testimony. I remember being rather more nervous than usual, blushing my way through Malcolm's introduction until, at last, I was left there on my own to get on with it.

Not wanting to look foolish, I composed myself as much as I could and just began to talk. I told them where I was from and who my family were, about the drinking and the drug taking, my descent into drug dealing and the trouble it caused, right up until it all ended rather unglamorously with a failed suicide attempt in March 2006, a trip back to Shetland and a stay in rehab.

From the very outset, the nervousness I suffered was almost crippling, the inward struggle to speak on those very delicate subjects almost too much for me to bear – until I began to speak about the experience on Papa Stour. Immediately, everything began to change, as what felt like a wave washed over me, completely removing all fear. I remember pausing momentarily – not quite sure what to make of it – then taking a sip of water and a deep breath, as the words that flowed from my lips seemed to take on a life of their own. And so it was that, at that exact moment, I finally thought I understood what this "authority" I had been given was; it was what Scripture called the Holy Spirit!

Amazed at such a revelation, and filled with a tremendous sense of confidence, I suddenly found myself preaching on chapter 20 of John's Gospel, explaining how those verses led me to a heightened sense of conviction for the kind of life that I had lived, and how that ultimately caused me to cry out to God for forgiveness.

The room, at that point, was electric. No one moved. Not a sound was made. All eyes were fixed firmly on me, some with a look of excitement, some trying hard to hold back tears, and some obviously not succeeding. Then, as I concluded with how He had "heard my cry, answered my prayer and set me free", cries of "Praise God" and "Thank You, Jesus" accompanied a hearty, wall-trembling applause, the likes of which I had never experienced before.

This, I very quickly understood, was what it was all about; publicly testifying of Him, of what He had done for me, with this amazing gift of divine authority, which I realised was God's Spirit within me.

Sverrir, who had been sitting in the third row next to my aunt Margaret, simply nodded his head and winked with one of his "see, I told you so" looks, with which I had become so familiar.

In the days and weeks that followed, I received many an invitation to share my testimony, some from local churches and some from private prayer meetings. I was even invited, on a few occasions, to talk in people's homes. It really was astonishing, and I had quite honestly never felt happier or that my life had ever had so much purpose – until an invitation arrived asking me to begin the treatment for hep C, which in the midst of all the excitement had somehow managed to slip my mind.

During this period of speaking engagements I had, to a certain degree, almost managed to forget what was going on inside me, but then, it wasn't something I shared when giving my testimony. I would talk about life after Papa

Stour and how different it was from before, but concerning my health, I was always more than vague.

If I was offered prayer at the end of a talk, for instance, which I soon discovered was normal practice, I would merely mention "a little problem with my liver" and let whoever wanted to pray about it pray as they felt led. There just didn't seem to be any sense of urgency, or worry even; that same old PJ was surfacing once more, the one who had always believed that ignorance was bliss.

The sudden arrival of that particular invitation, however, quickly brought me back down to earth, and on Friday, 12 January, 2007, I attended my first appointment at Woolmanhill Hospital in Aberdeen.

* * *

As much as I had been looking forward to commencing the treatment, being back in Aberdeen came as something of a shock. From the moment I stepped off the airplane I was completely on edge, constantly looking over my shoulder, scrutinising anyone and everyone who came my way.

To begin with I couldn't quite work out why I was feeling like that, and it really bothered me. I mean, it wasn't as if I had any dealings with anyone in Aberdeen, and certainly no one knew I would be arriving there; nevertheless, I felt extremely vulnerable, almost to the point where I thought I might have a panic attack.

As I made my way to the bus stop, I tried to calm myself and make some sense of it, and then I realised something quite disturbing. My very existence had been in serious jeopardy prior to my leaving Aberdeen, and what I had experienced stepping from the plane was merely an indication of just how dangerous that life had actually been. Of course, I'd always been too drunk every day to realise it, or worse still, perhaps, even care.

Yes, it really was a frightening thought and one that I didn't particularly welcome, although it was an excellent reminder of just how much my circumstances had changed. Just as important, it proved without a shadow of doubt that leaving Aberdeen when I did had been the right decision at the right time.

I arrived at the clinic, somewhat relieved, almost two hours after landing, made myself known at the reception desk and wandered off into the waiting area, glad to be off the streets.

Able to relax at last, I sat peacefully skimming through the pages of some magazines, lifting my head every now and then as people came and went, until my attention was drawn to various posters on a faraway wall.

The posters themselves were nothing more than one would expect to find in a place like that, but what bothered me on closer inspection was that every single one of them – either subtly or completely in your face – seemed to relate to me, almost as if they had been deliberately chosen for my visit. There were some on the dangers of certain drugs and the effects they can have on your mental and physical wellbeing; there were some on the dangers of sharing needles and other such paraphernalia, like spoons and filters; there were some on the dangers of unprotected sex and the various diseases you might pick up and, of course, there were some with information on how to seek help and which support groups were available, if you happened to think you were at risk!

As I read each one, this anger seemed to well up within me. My cheeks began to burn with embarrassment, as that diseased blood of mine pumped faster and faster through my body, my heart racing.

Yes, those posters certainly brought out a reaction in me, but there was one in particular which – although very simple and none too graphic – seemed to disturb me more than any other. It had a picture of a filthy syringe drawing up from an even filthier spoon!

How many times have you seen that same sight, Peter? I mentally scolded myself. *How many times have you done that and worse, you idiot?*

I just couldn't believe I was sitting there looking at all that stuff on the wall, which to most people was common sense. Yet, there I was, a middle-aged man about to start a programme for hep C! Where was the sense in that?

Relieved to finally hear my name called, I was led at last from the waiting area to one of the consultation rooms.

Sally, who would be directing the programme, quickly introduced herself, as well as one or two other people in the room, and explained why I was there and what I could expect over the next few months.

I listened as best I could to all she had to tell me and although greatly disappointed to learn that it would be another four months before the actual treatment would begin, I was pleased that things were finally moving forward. Sally then explained the significance of meeting with me first and running a few more tests, the most important of which was to find out the exact strain of the virus.

Having become used to procedures of this kind, I accepted what I had been told and then obligingly did everything that was asked of me. I stood on the scales so they could weigh me, stuck out my arm so they could take more bloods, answered this question and that question, signed this document after that document, and all the while, as they ran one little test after another, I hardly said a word.

"So, Peter, why don't you tell us a little about yourself?" Sally said, at last.

Well, needless to say I couldn't help myself, and with God's Holy Spirit waiting patiently in the wings for such an opportune moment, I delivered a scaled-down version of my testimony, concluding it rather unconventionally, perhaps, by sticking my hand inside the collar of my shirt and proudly producing a little wooden cross (a present from Brother Clifford), which I began to wave around.

"And I have all these people praying for me!" I informed her. "They're praying that I'll be completely healed."

It certainly wasn't what she'd been expecting to hear from a man as quiet as I'd been throughout, and it definitely raised quite a laugh amongst us, even prompting a genuine interest to find out more. But once again it completely blew away all fear, reminding me instantly of Who was in control.

Yes, visiting Aberdeen had been an experience I wasn't quite prepared for. Old wounds had been opened up, with things that had been buried deep surfacing once more, reminding me of what life had been like, the many mistakes I had made and how lucky I was to have gotten out of there alive. I was told I would start the treatment in four months' time and trips to Aberdeen – possibly every week, certainly every month – were something I'd just have to get used to.

Now, having been reminded of just how empty, how shallow, in fact, how utterly dangerous my past life had been, I actually found that I couldn't wait for the treatment to begin – especially for that glorious day when it was finally over and I could hopefully put it all behind me once and for all. And for that I was extremely thankful.

* * *

Thinking everything had gone reasonably well in Aberdeen, and that all I had to do was wait for the treatment to start, I was mystified a few days later when I received a letter requesting me to attend my local hospital in Lerwick for a liver scan.

I have to admit that up until then I hadn't really given the matter too much thought. Even the trip to Woolmanhill Hospital hadn't exactly spurred me into any sense of urgency; in fact, I had become quite flippant, until, all of a sudden, it stood like a mighty mountain across my path.

Standing there in the middle of the living room with that piece of paper in my hand, it became clear to me that it required some serious consideration. More than anything, it required some serious prayer, and I had sorely neglected both these things concerning this particular issue.

Over the previous three or four months I had all but removed the matter from my mind, only ever touching on it briefly when sharing my testimony, but never once mentioning that I was hep C positive. I suppose I was just too caught up in the excitement of what was going on around me to give it the respect it deserved, brushing it aside as if it were nothing more serious than a common cold.

Then, all of a sudden, there it was staring me right in the face: not a disease that might affect my blood and liver to some insignificant degree, but a killer virus that would without mercy cut short my life if not treated successfully. I decided it was time to take action, turned my attention to prayer, and sought the counsel of those few Christians who were in the know.

A couple of nights later, having received some spiritual advice, I went to a mid-week meeting at the church I was attending, which just happened to be on intercessory prayer – the very thing I was told I needed. As the meeting drew to a close, Steve Wright, one of the church leaders, asked me how things had gone in Aberdeen and if I needed prayer for anything specific.

The truth was there on the tip of my tongue and I dearly wanted to blurt it out to him – but again, I just couldn't say the words.

"Och, they want me to have a liver scan in a few days' time, and I'm a little worried and confused as to why!" was all I managed to disclose.

Steve looked at me for a little while, as people gathered round, then as others began praying out in what sounded like a foreign language (something I always found rather amusing), he began to pray in a way quite unlike anyone had prayed for me before.

"Dear heavenly Father, we thank You for our dear brother, Pete – that You, in your love for him, have lifted him out of darkness and into the glorious light of knowing You. It is our prayer tonight that as Pete goes for this scan on His liver, You will perform a miracle that won't only fill Pete with wonder and amazement, but more than anything will bring glory to You in that hospital. May they discover that Pete's liver has been healed *in Jesus' name*!"

"Yes," I agreed, "for Your glory, Lord."

I stood there, listening to those who had gathered round as they took turns to pray for me, and I couldn't help but be touched by Steve's words – and what's more, I chose to believe them.

Two days later I was at the hospital sitting in another waiting area. I picked up a magazine then quickly browsed the walls for any interesting posters, until a little later a lady in white overalls popped her head around the corner and called out in a gentle Irish accent.

"Peter Jamieson? This way, please."

I followed her down the corridor and into a large room filled with monitors and pieces of hi-tech equipment.

"Hi, Peter, my name is Clare, and I will be the one scanning your, eh ... What is it you're having done again? Oh, yes, your liver!" she said, laughing.

Looking a little embarrassed, she instructed me to strip to my waist, lie down and relax. Sitting down next to me, she then applied a gel-like substance to the area she wanted to scan, turned the monitor round so that it faced her, and began running this cold piece of equipment back and forth across my midriff.

Unable to see the screen, I lay there listening to the clicks of the device as she took various shots of my liver, worrying to myself what it might look like.

And then, as if on cue, she piped up, "So, Peter, tell me a little about yourself and how you come to be here."

Well, needless to say, I proceeded to share my testimony.

Clare listened to my story, while at the same time clicking away at my liver, acknowledging her interest now again with the occasional, "Oh, yeah?" and "Uh, huh!"

"And now I'm a born-again Christian," I eventually concluded. "And do you know what? I have all these people praying for me, and they're all praying that I'll be completely healed!"

Expecting her to laugh, I twisted my head round so that I could at least see her expression. But she didn't laugh; in fact, she looked quite serious.

"Well, Peter," she said, "I'd tell them to keep it up, if I were you, because it's obviously doing something."

"What do you mean?" I asked, straining my neck to make eye contact.

Having taken enough shots of my liver, Clare invited me to turn over so that I could have a look for myself. She moved the scanning apparatus across my side with one hand, while pointing at the screen with her other.

"You see that there, Peter? That's your liver and as far as appearance goes, it looks perfectly healthy to me!"

"What?" I gasped. "Well, that's really good, isn't it?"

Clare laughed. "To be perfectly honest, I was expecting to see little lumps and scars all over the surface, but there are none – none whatsoever!"

I could feel goose bumps forming on the back of my neck, excitement rising up within me.

"But this is the bit that really gets me ..." she said, pointing to a small area on my liver and making circular movements around it. "You see this piece here that looks a little like a valve, where it looks like the blood is going in and out? Well, this is where I was expecting to find at least some degree of damage, especially considering your history."

Clare fell silent for a moment or two, and took a few more shots. "But there's no sign of any damage, whatsoever. Peter, your liver looks perfectly healthy."

I honestly couldn't believe what I was hearing.

"Wow, that's really good, isn't it?" I exclaimed, and we both laughed.

Clare then handed me a towel to wipe away the remainder of the gel.

"Peter, all I can say is you must just be a really healthy guy!" she said, as she flicked off the monitor.

"What? Healthy? *Me*?"

I certainly never expected to hear that said in my lifetime.

She walked over to her computer, sat down and began looking over the various shots of my liver in preparation to send them off to Aberdeen.

"Clare, can I ask you something?" I asked, as I prepared to leave the room.

She turned to look at me. "Yes, of course."

"See what you saw on that screen ...? Were you at all surprised by any of it?"

Clare considered for a moment.

"Over the years I have had women come in here who have never had a drink in their lives and whose livers don't look as healthy as yours. Yes, you could say I am surprised."

With unimaginable joy spread clearly across my face, I quickly responded.

"That, Clare, is the power of prayer."

Clare smiled, nodding her head a little.

"Well, I'm not going to argue with you there!"

* * *

On Friday, 27 May, at roughly 10 o'clock in the evening, I finally began the treatment for hep C. Sitting up in my bed, the device used to inject the peginterferon in one hand, and a lump of flab where I would administer the first dose in the other, I nervously brought the point of the needle down, while at the same time calling out, "Okay, God, *this is it!*"

Injecting the contents of that pen into my belly, although somewhat satisfying, was the beginning of what might easily have been a very tough time. In fact, a book given to me at the clinic had described the various side effects most commonly suffered with this form of chemotherapy, and they certainly weren't anything to look forward to: hair loss, weight loss, depression, headaches, nausea, vomiting ...

The list just went on and on, describing some 50 or so possible nasties, the most worrying of which were undoubtedly "suicidal thoughts" and "completion of suicide". No, it certainly wasn't to be taken lightly.

However, I was highly confident that it wouldn't be anywhere near as bad as that for me, and with very good reason, too, I felt. The results of a blood test had revealed a factor that weighed very heavily in my favour, which I believed was yet another answer to prayer. It turned out that I had the No. 3 strain of the virus, which Sally reckoned was quite rare in drug addicts, who were more likely to have the No. 1 strain. In her experience that was by far the worst.

The No. 3 strain, which everyone at the clinic had been pleasantly surprised by, was said to be the easiest of the six known strains of the virus to eradicate, with an impressive 75% pass rate. Also, having the No.3 strain meant that I faced six months of treatment, rather than a whole year.

Okay, it still meant that I had to undergo the treatment, which wasn't something to look forward to, whatever the strain, but I certainly felt justified in being so hopeful. I trusted in a God who was bigger than any human frailty, disease or pesky virus, and whatever I might suffer as a result, even if I had a touch of every side effect imaginable, I certainly wasn't going to suffer from the fear of it. God, I believed, was firmly in control – no matter how hard the treatment, no matter the outcome.

The first week or so of treatment passed without too much fuss. After injecting myself with the interferon alpha on the Friday night, and then taking the ribaviron tablets twice daily after that, other than suffering with what felt very much like an alcohol-induced hangover, by Monday morning I felt fine. Work, as well as my many other social engagements, hopefully wasn't going to pose too much of a problem.

As time progressed, however, I detected a certain air of depression directly after injecting myself on Friday nights, which seemed to last that little bit longer each time, stretching farther out into the next week. I tried not to let this bother me and watched to see if things improved.

At the end of the first full month I was flown back to Aberdeen – my third trip in approximately 28 days – for a more thorough check-up than previously. I went through the usual rigmarole of tests, with one or two new ones thrown in for good measure, and other than losing about 4 kg in weight, they seemed pleased with how well I was holding out. This resulted in my being allocated enough medication to last me 28 days instead of 14, something I was very grateful for.

I had felt a little rough all right, there was no question about that, but I didn't tell them to what extent in case they decided to put me back on a two-week programme. They were just so pleased with my progress, and I was just happy to get out of there with one less trip to Aberdeen every month, that any concerns I may have had, rightly or wrongly, I kept very much to myself.

Later that evening I returned home to Scalloway, made some room in my fridge for a month's worth of treatment, and considered the prospect of another five months of feeling like I did, or perhaps even worse.

Should I have told them how I was really feeling? I wondered. *Will I have to give up my employment as a result? Will I become housebound?*

These were questions that needed some serious thought, as the consequences were very real.

That night, as I lay in bed preparing to administer the next dose of interferon, I set the pen down on my bedside table and this time I poured out my heart to God, asking Him to help me through the worst of it. Satisfied that I had said all I needed to say, I then injected myself once more, set the needle down and turned out my light.

Some hours later I suddenly woke with a start. The room was pitch dark, all was silent, all was still; in the hallway outside my bedroom door, on the winding staircase, on the old wooden floorboards, not a sound could be heard, but as I lay sleeping I had heard a voice clearly speaking to me – loud enough that it had made me sit bolt upright in my bed.

I sat there in the dark for a while, listening to the silence of that old, seafront house, wondering who or what it could have been, and if I might hear anything else, but the darkness wasn't very forthcoming and so eventually I lay down once more and thought instead about what I had heard. It had been a man's voice – an extremely powerful, yet very gentle voice – that simply said, as if speaking right from within me, "Proverbs 25, verse 16."

A little startled at the intrusion, I finally fell asleep.

The following morning I awoke at seven, snoozed on and off for half an hour, then dragging myself out of bed I wandered off down the old wooden staircase to where Andy and Sabina, who had come out of Papa Stour for the weekend, sat eating their breakfast. With my duvet wrapped around me, I wished them both "Good morning", lay down on the sofa and waited for the expected "hangover" to eventually catch up with me.

"So, how are you feeling this Saturday morning?" Sabina asked.

"Mmm, yeah, not too sure ... Probably not very good," I replied.

Sabina was sitting at the dining table eating her boiled eggs and toast, watching me over the top of her glasses.

"Pete," she began, in a tone that usually implied a lecture was coming, "how on earth are you managing to survive? There's nothing of any nutritional value in your cupboards. I've just had a look and it's all complete rubbish! Pasta 'n' Sauce, Pot Noodles, crisps ...? Is that what you've been living on for the last few weeks? It's hardly surprising you're losing weight. You need to eat proper food, Pete, not that junk!"

Sabina was very outspoken when it came to so-called "healthy eating", which was something I found hard to deal with at times, especially being a middle-aged man and perfectly able to decide those things for myself.

I shut her out momentarily – as was sometimes necessary – and gazed out of the window at the sea.

"Pete, are you even listening to me? I'm telling you this for your own good, you know."

I turned and looked at her.

"Yeah, I'm listening."

"Right, Pete, this is what we'll do. I'm going into Lerwick shortly to do some shopping, and while I'm there I'll buy you some honey. Do you like honey?"

I nodded.

"Good, then I will buy you some honey. And what you'll need to do is mix a couple of spoonfuls in a cup, pour in a splash of cider vinegar, mix it up with some hot water and then drink it. It really is very good for you, Pete."

I sat there looking at her, speechless.

"Will you do that?" she asked. "Will you promise to drink this honey if I buy it for you? It really is very good for you!"

If the side effects of the interferon weren't yet making me ill, Sabina going on at me – especially at that time in the morning – was having a very similar effect!

"Now, Pete ..."

"Sabina, okay! I hear what you're saying! Yes, I'll drink the blooming stuff!" I snapped.

Sabina began to blush, making me feel guilty.

"Look, I'm sorry, Sabina, I didn't mean to be rude. It's just this treatment ..."

"Yes, I know, and that is why I am telling you this. It's for your *own good!*"

She always had to get the last word.

I lay there looking out of the window, watching a couple of yachts berthing at the boating club marina, with thoughts of a long day ahead almost bringing a tear to my eye. Not even Sverrir was around anymore to brighten things up, his time in Shetland having come to an end.

Then suddenly I remembered the voice.

"Sabina ... I heard a voice speaking to me in my sleep. It woke me up!"

"What did it say?"

"It just said 'Proverbs 25, verse 16'. Is there such a thing?" I asked.

Sabina passed me a Bible. "Yes, I'm sure there is."

I promptly sat upright on the sofa, opened up the Bible and began skimming through the pages until I reached the book of Proverbs. Quickly locating chapter 25, I ran my finger down the page until it sat at verse 16, and on reading it I couldn't help but laugh out loud, the Bible almost falling from my lap onto the floor.

"What is it? What does it say?" Sabina had been surprised by my outburst and sat there, a confused look on her face, which made it all the funnier.

"Sabina, you're not going to believe this." I forced myself to stop laughing, so I could read it to her. "Proverbs 25, verse 16 says: 'If you have found honey, eat only enough for you, lest you have your fill of it and vomit it'."

I laughed again until tears rolled down my cheeks, knowing that God had clearly spoken to me in my sleep, while at the same time revealing His wonderful sense of humour.

Sabina didn't share the fun in quite the same way.

"You made that up!" she scoffed.

I immediately handed her the Bible, and watched her as she read it, a smile slowly breaking across her face.

* * *

The anticipated "hangover", which eventually came, never seemed to bother me much after that. In fact, for the majority of the time from that day on I was unaware of any side effects. The depression that had been threatening to engulf me, I could turn to joy, and if I happened to feel a little ill – which was rare – I rejoiced knowing that God was fully aware of how I was feeling and what's more, that He cared.

I carried on with the treatment for the remaining five months, constantly surprising everyone by the sheer lack of side effects, an absolute picture of health right up until it finished in November.

Of course, the big test came six months after the treatment was complete; if the results of that blood test were still clear, it was then and only then that I would be classed as officially hep C free.

On Monday, 2 June, 2008, almost two years to the day since I left Papa Stour, I received the letter declaring me as such. It was a momentous occasion as far as I was concerned, especially considering how different things might have turned out had I not sought the help I needed when I did.

Yes, things could have ended up very different. But Someone, thankfully, had another design for my life, one that I could fully trust in.

* * *

Walking away from that dental practice in Lerwick the very next day – when at last I had been able to fill in that form with the information that I was, indeed, hep C free – with a mouth full of novocaine, the sun beating down and a joy in my heart like that of a child, I knew how blessed I had been.

Living a lie had almost destroyed me, but by finally surrendering all that was in my heart – those beliefs that made me who I was – and by looking at myself in the only "Mirror" that will ever truly help us to see ourselves as we really are – the face of Jesus Christ Himself – was I able to be free of whatever it was that held me captive all those years.

So, what was it that had the power to take such control of my life? What was it that required me to put my trust in Jesus to finally break its hold?

I remember, as a child of perhaps three years, waking in the early hours of the morning in a fit of complete terror.

Directly outside my bedroom window I saw, against the gentle hue of a dawn sky, a dark foreboding entity seemingly searching for a way in. I had no idea what it was at the time, but I somehow knew that it wanted to reach me; I knew also, as unrecognisable as it may have been, that it was the essence of pure evil.

As I sat upright in my bed, pointing towards the window with one very small, outstretched hand, crying hysterically, with a feeling of suffocation, as the air I breathed seemed putrid, I had watched with fear as it hovered outside, desperately hoping that it wouldn't find a way in to me. But, eventually, it did.

I have thought about that experience many times, as the memory of it has never left me, and over the years have had many different ideas as to what it could have been. As a child growing up and encountering movies, for instance, I used to think of it as some kind of monster, although certainly worse than anything that man's imagination could muster. Then as a teenager, with a strong belief in the supernatural, it changed to something of a demonic nature, especially after the séance and the consequences that quickly followed. Even as an adult going through the trials of addiction and depression, I firmly believed that something very powerful had always had a hold on me, and no matter what, it would never let go. Whatever it was that had been at my window, that far away morning, many years ago, had never left me.

Since encountering Christ, however, and reading His life-giving Word in the Bible, I have, of course, found the identity of my dawn visitor, and it wasn't quite what I had thought, but something fully worse.

The Gospel of John, tells us that the devil is a deceiver, the "father of lies" (John 8:44) who wants only to "steal and kill and destroy" (John 10:10). And he did. With his hand upon me from a very young age, he stole my life from me; of that, nothing can be surer.

Walking along that road on my way to where my sister worked to share with her the good news of the results, my heart was filled to overflowing with something that from earliest memory I had somehow learned to live without. Now it coursed through me, its power conquering all in its path, renewing and refreshing this once darkened mind, opening my eyes to the wonder of life. Yes, this thing that now lived within me, which in the blink of an eye had shattered to smithereens every conceivable lie I ever believed about myself and at the same time loosed me from the tenacious grip of that which only ever wanted to blind me from the truth, was a thing called love.

How blind I had been, how wrong I had been, how easily fooled I had been, all the while rejecting the possibility that there was a God who loved me and only wanted the best for me. In my close-mindedness I had simply refused to consider this, as the world around me only spoke of hurt, pain and rejection, which was, of course, easily bolstered by various world events and society in general.

Who would have created such an awful place as this, surely not all powerful, all knowing, all loving God? But, thankfully, my eyes were opened, and love, the most powerful thing in the entire universe, won the day: the love of my heavenly Father, the Lord God Jesus Christ.

"Amazing grace, how sweet the sound
that saved a wretch like me.
I once was lost, but now am found,
was blind, but now I see."

Taken from the hymn "Amazing Grace"
by John Newton.

EPILOGUE

If you have reached this far in the book, I really must commend you. Not having done anything of this nature before, I know how much it may lack in a literary sense. For all I know, there may have been times when you've wondered if you would ever finish it, such has been your frustration! But the fact that you have stayed with me this long must show that you were at least a little interested in what I had to say, reading onwards towards the end, perhaps, with a glimmer of hope that it might lead you down a similar path, or at the very least answer some of those questions you've been harbouring about God.

So, how do I go about tying up the story in a way that will, hopefully, leave you feeling satisfied, after having painstakingly worked your way through it?

Since accepting Jesus as my Lord and Saviour, life has been one roller coaster of a ride. I have been blessed many times by how God has led me, communicated with me, and revealed Himself to me, but the most important thing of all is what He has promised awaits me when my time on this earth reaches its end: eternal life (1 John 2:25).

The things of God that I have experienced so far – and only a very small percentage are included in this book – are all precious to me, and I am sure you'll agree they are quite astounding. However, it's God's promise of Salvation that I'm most grateful for, and that's what I hope you, the reader, if you are not already "saved", will also choose. Realising your need to be saved is the greatest revelation that you could ever have, and accepting God's gift of Salvation is the most important decision you will ever make. But will you?

The aim of this book, strange as it may seem, isn't to convince you to do this, rather it is to hopefully make you think about your own life, past and present, and ultimately what lies beyond it.

Every person who has ever lived has a story to tell, after all, but it's my belief that for many that story is, and will remain, largely incomplete – until they too discover the true meaning of their existence.

So, does the universe exist because of a mere accident? Is biological life simply the result of a haphazard accumulation of chemicals that got lucky in some pond, once upon a time? Or are we, as the Bible says, the creation of a supernatural being Who had each one of us in mind before the universe even began?

These are questions that people/scientists constantly struggle to answer, and it seems the more they search for what they hope will put an end to a supernatural cause, the more difficult that struggle becomes.

For me, that particular struggle – along with the many other struggles I have encountered throughout my life – no longer exists, because the Creator of everything, of all that is, one day became real to me, and what I hope this book does, more than anything, is testify to this: God is real.

As the reader of this book, I suppose you now have to make up your mind. Does God really exist? Is there really such a thing as eternal life? As I said earlier, it's not my intention to try to convince you one way or the other, but knowing what I do, it is my prayer that you'll give it serious consideration, because there really is so much at stake.

As I type, I can't help but think of my own journey to Salvation and how thankful I am for having made that decision; it really could have been so different. What if that young man from Elim Church hadn't visited what was one of the hardest bars in Aberdeen at that time as often as he did? What if he hadn't taken time to get to know me? What if I'd not prayed following the attempted suicide? What if Aaron Irvine, who I've mentioned in chapters eight and nine, hadn't bothered to tell me about the Papa Stour Project?

Yes, I truly am thankful that, for once in my life, I made some good decisions, and I truly do believe that God used all those things, and probably a lot more besides, to eventually draw me out of the darkness and into the light.

Perhaps, then, this book is a part of your journey, maybe it's one of those little signposts that God is using to direct you back to Him?

Well, I suppose there's only one way to find out, isn't there? If you would like to take that first step towards receiving eternal life, then you can begin it right now by saying this very simple prayer:

> *"Dear God in heaven, I come to you in the name of Jesus. I acknowledge before You now that I am a sinner, and that I need Your forgiveness. I believe that Your only begotten Son, Jesus Christ, shed His precious blood on the cross at Calvary and died for my sins, and I am now willing to turn from my sinful ways.*
>
> *"Your Holy Word says, in Romans 10:9, that if we confess Jesus Christ as Lord, and believe in our hearts that God raised Him from the dead, we shall be saved. Right now, I confess Jesus as the Lord of my soul. With my heart, I believe that God raised Jesus from the dead and from this very moment I accept Jesus Christ as my own personal Saviour, and that according to His Word I am saved. Thank you, Jesus, for dying for me and for Your promise of eternal life.*
>
> *"Please now send Your Holy Spirit to be my guide and teacher, to help me obey You and do Your will for the rest of my life. Amen."*

If you have said this prayer, I would advise you to contact a local Christian church, or someone you know who is a true Christian, and explain to them what you have done and why. They should be able to point you in the right direction, as to how you should go forward in this wonderful new life that you have chosen. Congratulations, you are now born again.

Enjoy the journey, and whatever comes your way!

Peter Jamieson

For further information or copies of *Design for Life*, or to make a donation towards the work of Aald Rock Ministries, please contact:

Aald Rock Ministries
Seaview House
Main Street
Scalloway
Shetland Isles
ZE1 0XJ

Tel: 01959 880900

Email: peter.jamieson@inbox.com